A Report On a Preliminary Survey of Certain Departments of the City of Milwaukee

CONTENTS

282076

FOREWORD

The New York Bureau of Municipal Research is a private organization supported by citizens of that city to promote efficiency and economy in city government. For eight years past this unofficial Bureau, through a trained, permanent staff, has coöperated with the municipal officials of Greater New York in organizing and modernizing that city's administrative practices. This Bureau has not only accomplished splendid results, but has kept the public fully informed as to the facts concerning the city's business.

Following the example of New York, citizens of Philadelphia, Cincinnati, Chicago, Portland, Ore., and elsewhere have established similar bureaus to improve the government of their own cities by means of continuous coöperation between citizens and city officials in instituting practices of efficiency.

A group of citizens in Milwaukee have for some time felt that a citizens' bureau modeled on the plan of the New York Bureau of Municipal Research would be of service in helping to bring about more efficient government in this city. An independent and permanent Milwaukee citizens' bureau would insure the general efficiency of the city's government regardless of political or administrative changes. In order that a local bureau might be established with definite understanding of the city's present administrative conditions, the New York Bureau of Municipal Research was employed to make a preliminary survey of the city's government. In this undertaking the committee first sought and secured the most cordial coöperation of the mayor and the city's officials.

The survey was made in April, 1913, the report of which is herewith submitted. Many of the recommendations contained in the report have been anticipated by the present city government, and some have already been adopted. When all are carried out, the committee feels assured that there will have been established in Milwaukee, methods of administration equal in effectiveness to those found anywhere in the cities of the United States.

C. NESBITT DUFFY
ALBERT FRIEDMANN
WALTER STERN
Committee

LETTER TO MAYOR FROM COMMITTEE OF
CITIZENS TRANSMITTING REPORT

July 17, 1913

To the Honorable Dr. G. A. BADING,
  Mayor, City of Milwaukee,
    Milwaukee, Wisconsin.

DEAR SIR:

The undersigned committee, having in charge the inauguration of the proposed Milwaukee Citizens' Bureau of Municipal Efficiency, takes pleasure in presenting to you herewith the report of the preliminary survey of the government of the city of Milwaukee, as made by the New York Bureau of Municipal Research, together with certain suggestions and recommendations for increasing the efficiency of Milwaukee's city government. We wish to call your attention to the fact that since this report was written, several of the suggestions and recommendations as enumerated therein have been acted upon by some of the departments.

It is especially gratifying to note that so much in the present administration of the city's affairs is so highly commended. It is also gratifying to have recorded the indorsement of the work accomplished and the program of the work undertaken by the bureau of municipal research, which you inaugurated under the direction of Mr. Ralph Bowman.

It is now the intention to complete the arrangements for establishing the Milwaukee Citizens' Bureau of Municipal Efficiency, which has received your hearty indorsement, and which we believe will be an important factor in contributing toward greater efficiency in Milwaukee's city government. We trust you will feel free to call upon the Bureau for such assistance and coöperation as it may be able to render and will be glad to extend the city administration.

5

We desire to emphasize our appreciation of the courtesies extended to the New York Bureau in making the preliminary survey of the government of the city of Milwaukee, as well as the undersigned committee, in your sincere desire to aid in the movement to improve Milwaukee's municipal affairs.

Respectfully,

C. NESBITT DUFFY
ALBERT FRIEDMANN
WALTER STERN
Committee

MAYOR'S REPLY TO COMMITTEE OF CITIZENS

July 18, 1913

MESSRS. C. NESBITT DUFFY, ALBERT FRIEDMANN and
WALTER STERN, Committee,
Milwaukee.

GENTLEMEN:

I desire to acknowledge receipt of the report of the preliminary survey of the government of the city of Milwaukee as made by the New York Bureau of Municipal Research, at your suggestion.

In reading this report, I note with a great deal of satisfaction and pleasure the indorsement of the program by the New York Bureau, as well as the work so far undertaken and accomplished by the present administration toward placing the city government on a higher basis of efficiency. A certain number of the suggestions and recommendations have already been covered in the various departments they refer to, and others are in process of undertaking. In numerous instances it will be necessary to secure legislative action before changes recommended can be carried out. On the whole, the suggestions and recommendations made are acceptable to the administration, and will, no doubt, in due course of time, be followed.

I have indorsed the establishment of the Milwaukee Citizens'

6

Bureau of Municipal Efficiency because it is my desire to make use of any and every agency tending to assist this administration in giving to the people of our city an efficient and economical administration and form of government. I will therefore avail myself of the opportunity, in case the Citizens' Bureau becomes a reality, to call upon it for such assistance and coöperation as it may be able to render to the administration, and again assure you of the full coöperation not only of myself but also of the various heads of departments of my administration.

Thanking you, I am,

Very respectfully,

G. A. BADING,
Mayor

LETTER OF TRANSMITTAL

June 2, 1913

Messrs. C. NESBITT DUFFY, ALBERT FRIEDMANN
and WALTER STERN,
Milwaukee, Wisconsin.

GENTLEMEN:

At your request the New York Bureau of Municipal Research has made a brief, preliminary survey of the government of the city of Milwaukee and begs herewith to submit its report.

This survey was undertaken with the following purposes in view:

1. To learn the existing important administrative problems confronting the government of the city
2. To formulate a plan for constructive coöperation between the city government and a proposed Milwaukee Citizens' Bureau of Municipal Efficiency

You did not request that an exhaustive study be made, but that so far as possible, in the brief time available, a definite picture be obtained of existing administrative conditions in the city government.

Effective Efficiency Work Already Begun

On January 1, 1913, at the request of Mayor Bading, the Training School for Public Service of the New York Bureau of Municipal Research sent Mr. Ralph Bowman to Milwaukee to organize a bureau of municipal research as a part of the mayor's office. This bureau had been in operation for three months at the time of our survey and with the active coöperation of city officials had already effectively begun the application of a program of municipal efficiency, such as the New York Bureau of Municipal Research has suggested and applied in other cities.

As the following report will point out, Milwaukee, despite handicaps of compulsory charter provisions and complicated administrative organization, is in an exceptionally favorable position to establish the government of the city upon an efficient business basis. The two most important offices of the city government, the offices of the mayor and the comptroller, have combined on a constructive program whose execution will place Milwaukee in the front rank of American municipalities in respect of efficient administration.

Cordial Coöperation of Officials

The New York Bureau of Municipal Research is greatly indebted to his Honor, Mayor Bading, to Mr. Ralph Bowman, director of the mayor's bureau, and to Mr. A. P. Puelicher, deputy comptroller, for their helpful coöperation in the survey. Every city official interviewed extended the representatives of the Bureau the most cordial courtesy, for which hearty and appreciative acknowledgment is here made.

Time Schedule of Survey

In order that the limitation of time in which the survey was made may be fully understood, we beg to present the following time schedule:

Our representatives arrived in Milwaukee on Monday afternoon, April 14th. Previously, on March 19th and 20th, a representative of the Bureau had reviewed the accounting methods of the city and conferred with the deputy comptroller on his plans for their reorganization.

Monday—April 14th, P. M. only

Two investigators

    Preliminary inspection of the city in an automobile

    Conference with the mayor and in the office of the bureau of municipal research

    Conference with the police chief

    Conference with the deputy comptroller

    Examination of charter and ordinances and budget and departmental reports

Tuesday—April 15th

Two investigators

    Department of public works, superintendent of street construction and repairs, deputy commissioner, chief clerk, purchasing agent, bureau of sanitation

    Police department

Wednesday—April 16th

Three investigators

    Field inspection of parks, streets, incinerator, and taking photographs of conditions observed

    Department of public works continued, bureau of sanitation, chief clerk

    City engineer's office, chief draughtsman

    City service commission

    Preparation of general organization chart of the city

    Department of health

Thursday—April 17th

Three investigators

    Department of public works continued, bureau of public buildings and bridges

    Department of health concluded

    Conference with various city officials to obtain data for and the completion of organization chart

    Summarizing results obtained to date, for conference with business men

    Conference with committee of citizens

    Dinner and evening meeting with business men

Friday—April 18th

Two investigators
Emergency hospital
Weights and measures
Park commission
City service commission
Police department concluded

Saturday—April 19th, A. M. only

Two investigators
Called on tax commisioner, treasurer, city clerk, etc.
Fire department
Meeting at city club

Tuesday—June 10th to Thursday—June 12th inc.

Two investigators
Checking and verifying draft report

Acknowledged Limitations of Results

Though obviously it was not possible in the time available for the survey to make a complete study of so extensive and intricate an organization as the government of Milwaukee, it was possible to learn, for the departments concerning which inquiry was made, where lie the greatest opportunities for constructive effort.

Accounting Reorganization Well in Hand

In this report only brief consideration will be given to accounting, record keeping and filing systems, for the reason that the deputy comptroller has undertaken a comprehensive reorganization of this part of the city's business methods.

Work Results Not Analyzed

No attempt was made to analyze the results of work performed by the departments surveyed. Attention was given exclusively to program, organization and method, with the presumption that a progressive program, efficient organization and efficient methods are likely to produce efficient results.

10

Method of Survey

In studying the departments of the city government a definite plan was pursued. Based upon its eight years' experience, the Bureau of Municipal Research has formulated for use in making surveys more than 1,500 questions which seek to bring out essential facts regarding what the departments do and how they do it. In making a survey the Bureau does not set up an ideal standard or imaginary picture of city government by which to test the city under examination. It seeks merely to learn whether methods employed are generally as effective as methods used in similar work of one or another American city.

So far as possible with the brief opportunity for study afforded us, constructive suggestions are offered whenever criticism is made.

Draft Report Submitted to Responsible Officials

This report in draft form was submitted to the mayor and to the heads of the several departments discussed. All statements of fact contained in the report as now presented, have been reviewed by these responsible officials in so far as they relate to their respective departments.

Exemplary Practices in Milwaukee

It is a notable fact that in practically every city studied, activities are found which have attained a higher degree of efficiency than is common elsewhere. A number of such activities were encountered in our survey of Milwaukee, and to them reference will be made in the body of this report.

We beg to make clear to you, however, that in this report we have aimed to call attention particularly to conditions which are susceptible of improvement. For this reason less attention is given to those conditions concerning which we have no constructive suggestions to offer.

Respectfully submitted,

New York Bureau of Municipal Research

SUMMARY OF CRITICISMS AND CONSTRUCTIVE SUGGESTIONS REQUIRING NO ORDINANCE OR CHARTER REVISION

Mayor

1. It is suggested that the mayor invite the members of the various boards and departments to meet with him periodically, in order to discuss and adopt a common administrative program affecting:

> a Central purchasing agency
> b Uniform system of accounts
> c Regular submission of departmental reports
> d Uniform working hours
> e Time reports
> f Uniform system of expense, stores and cost accounts
> g Uniform office rules and regulations
> h Standardization of departmental reports
> i Standardization of salaries
> j Centralized civil service control
> k Uniform efficiency records
> l Uniform system of promotion
> m Standardization of office equipment
> n Departmental conferences, educational courses for clerical force, etc.
> o Centralization of services wherever possible
> p Central bureau of information

Accounting

2. The deputy comptroller has outlined a plan for the comprehensive reorganization of the city's accounts. As yet, however, accounting methods throughout the departments are not standardized, nor has a complete modern system been installed in the comptroller's office. With the active coöperation of all departments notable progress may be expected in the city's accounting reorganization. No audits of departmental accounts are conducted, although they are now contemplated

Audit and Payment of Claims

3. The deputy comptroller recognizes the need of the following measures for improving the present audit procedure:

   a A complete contract file should be maintained in the comptroller's office and all contract payments carefully compared with contract provisions

   b Although the payroll audit is based on a card record similar to one kept by the city service commission, its accuracy is not verified by the comptroller. This should be done

   c Several departments do not keep time records to support their payrolls. Uniform time records should be installed

   d Payroll preparation and certificates are in urgent need of revision. Payrolls should be based on time reports certified by the employee himself or by his foreman. Payrolls should be certified by the person who prepares them as well as by the bureau head

   e Central control has not been established over financial stationery. Reports of collections, which should furnish a check on the treasurer, are not generally received

   f Control over collection of taxes in the comptroller's office is exercised only through the total amount of the tax roll. Tax bills should be made in multiple copies and a copy filed with the comptroller as a basis for auditing all collections

Budget Making

4. At present the accounts kept by the departments are of no value in preparing adequate budget estimates. The establishment of classified expense accounts, as planned by the comptroller, is therefore essential

5. A new law makes possible a budget expressing a specific, detailed program of activities and expenditures. Next

year's budget should have a summary showing total authorizations for all purposes according to departments and functions

Salary Standardization

6. It is usually desirable to have salary questions considered once a year. It is recommended that the council establish a rule that all requests for salary adjustments be submitted once a year by all departments unless it can be shown that an emergency exists

Department of Public Works

7. Clerical work of the department is not wholly centralized, the various bureaus having their own bookkeepers and clerks. With the possible exception of the water bureau, all bookkeeping should be done in the chief clerk's office
8. Payrolls for the several divisions are typewritten. Considerable time and expense would be saved if a mechanical process were used, similar to that employed in writing bills in the water department
9. Laborers are required to sign payrolls before actual payment of wages; this vitiates the value of receipt and should be discontinued
10. In many cases foremen write laborers' receipts. This should be immediately discontinued
11. The accounts of the department present with little exception a virgin field for constructive work. It is recommended that the deputy comptroller take up promptly a complete review of public works records
12. Ward superintendents and gang foremen are required to report time of members of gangs and character of work performed. These reports are not certified as correct. Foremen and ward superintendents should certify on all time reports that statements of fact contained therein are true

13. Uniform time reports should be provided for all labor forces

14. Clerical and supervisory employees should be required to submit weekly or semi-monthly statements of time and service

15. The monthly work reports submitted by ward superintendents of the division of street cleaning and garbage collection make no provision for certification by them as to accuracy of information contained therein. Such certification should be required

16. No provision is made for checking delivery of garbage, street sweepings, etc., to public dumps. The foreman who is stationed at each dump might readily report, by number, the wagons making deliveries

17. Permits for excavations, etc., are signed and issued to the applicant before payment of the required fee. A better procedure, and one which would eliminate the possibility of fraud, would be to require the applicant to file a receipt from the treasurer before the permit is issued to him

18. Stenographers are now attached to the several bureaus. A central stenographic bureau should be organized

19. The correspondence of the entire department should be filed in one central division

20. For files kept in the several divisions, a common system of classification and indexing should be adopted

Purchasing Division

21. The preceding administration established a complete register of vendors and a quotation register. Both these records have been permitted to lapse, though they constitute important accessories to efficient purchasing. They should be re-established

22. A current price record should be maintained, in order to comply with the ordinance and with good business practice

23. Buying is extensively done on open market orders, although the charter puts a limitation of $200 on open market purchases. It is entirely feasible to purchase most supplies on contract instead of on open market order

24. Supplies for storeroom purposes are bought on open market orders. Records of receipts and deliveries are maintained in the storeroom, so that there is no reason why contracts should not be entered into for storeroom supplies

25. Advantage has not been taken of the practice of combining into single contracts all supply and material requirements of a particular trade classification. The purchasing agent acts merely as a shopper for the several departments

26. Up to the time of this survey no analyses of kinds of supplies furnished nor attempt to forecast requirements had been made. The analysis of purchases of 1912 recently begun should furnish a basis for estimating requirements for the remainder of the present year and for 1914

27. Standards should be established and definite specifications prepared for all supplies regularly required

28. It is advantageous to make annual contracts at or about the beginning of the fiscal year. In case of coal and forage, short term agreements are preferable. In case of perishable food, monthly contracts should be made ·

29. Partial deliveries can be provided for in the contract

Bureau of Street Construction and Repair

30. Pavements under guarantee are generally repaired annually. Contractors should be required to maintain plants for repair of pavements throughout the year, or arrange with the city for their up-keep

31. A system of inspection should be established by the city for the prompt reporting of all pavement defects. For this purpose the city should be divided into districts and an inspector assigned to each district

32. The police may be utilized to report pavement defects
33. The department of public works should make a comprehensive study of prospective paving needs for a period of five years and a program of improvements should be determined on, according to which new construction work may be conducted
34. A definite policy should govern the determination of the kind of pavement to be laid on a particular street
35. Sub-surface maps should be prepared showing precise location and character of structures under the surface of streets
36. Street signs are inadequate. Good street signs are indispensable to strangers and a convenience to residents

Bureau of Sanitation

37. There are no definite standards for labor efficiency in the street cleaning department. Ward superintendents decide the fitness of the men under their supervision. The superintendent personally, or through a representative at the central office, should employ all laborers and assign them to the different wards
38. Rules for the guidance of all employees should be framed and a system of fines and penalties prescribed
39. Service records should be kept
40. The present tendency to regard the city payroll as a refuge for the indigent and infirm lowers the efficiency of service
41. Much time of laborers is wasted on pay day at the various ward yards. Payments should be made at places of work or at the beginning or close of day
42. Standards should be established for horses hired
43. The superintendent should control the maintenance and repair of city-owned equipment. It would probably be found profitable to establish a central repair shop or to have repairs made at one of the city shops already established. Ward superintendents should have no discretion in respect of these matters

44. The use of white uniforms should be made general throughout the city, and, if necessary, at the city's expense

45. Quarterly statements should be prepared showing cost and quantity of material and equipment used in the several wards, for purposes of comparison

46. Other statistical statements should be circulated for the information and stimulation of ward superintendents

47. Conferences between bureau superintendent and ward superintendents should be held from time to time

48. Tarpaulin covers should be promptly furnished for ash wagons. It might be feasible to adopt the type of ash wagon commonly used in German cities

49. Paved streets should be cleaned throughout the year

50. An adequate number of receptacles for sweepings should be placed on the streets at the beginning of the street cleaning season

51. Automobile trucks should be experimented with, to determine their usefulness

52. Household garbage should be collected more frequently than is now done

53. To standardize and increase the efficiency of street cleaning and garbage and ash collection, the superintendent should prepare and issue a definite set of departmental regulations which would prescribe in detail the duties of laborers and ward superintendents

Department of Bridges and Public Buildings

54. No record is kept of inspections made of buildings. A form for inspection should be prepared, and all public buildings should be subjected to examination once a year

55. Suitable cost records should be kept of repairs by departmental labor

56. Comparison of cost of cleaning public and private buildings would prove profitable

57. There should be regulations for cleaning buildings

58. The current generated in the lighting plant in City Hall building should be metered and careful records kept of operating cost to gauge efficiency of service

59. The problem of street lighting has been given little attention. Whether supplied by contract or by a city plant, supervision of location of lights and efficiency of service should be an important function of the bureau

60. Although an annual inventory is taken of equipment of buildings, neither the bureau nor the caretakers responsible are currently informed of what the property consists

61. City Hall should be provided with office directories on each floor

Police Department

62. The physical examination which candidates undergo before admission to the force should be paid for by the city

63. A medical examination of candidates should be given when the men first apply, instead of after they have passed other examinations

64. Standard notebooks should be provided for patrolmen. Sergeants and patrolmen should sign or initial each other's records

65. Patrolmen should not be permitted to exercise discretion in reporting violations of the law. If any class of violation is considered too trivial for report, this should be specifically stated

66. Standard forms should be provided for patrolmen's daily reports

67. Sergeants should make all reports in writing

68. According to a rule, which the chief states is not enforced, complaints received against members of the force are required to be signed. This rule should be modified to omit this provision. Anonymous complaints are valuable and should be encouraged

69. Complaints should be investigated by a confidential subordinate of the chief instead of the inspector

70. No officer found guilty of intoxication should be continued on the force. This practice is not always adhered to
71. "Look out" notices should be printed and distributed instead of read to the force
72. When persons called for are arrested, notice should be sent to officers
73. All patrolmen and detectives should be taught methods of identification from facial characteristics
74. Individual efficiency records are not kept. These records should be established for patrolmen and detectives
75. The percentage of children arrested shows the need of attention to recreation, home conditions, etc.
76. In its present form, the annual report cannot attain maximum usefulness:
    a It contains no textual matter, no review of improvements made, no suggestions for promoting efficiency. Program, probable needs and new undertakings should be discussed
    b No information is given of expenditures
    c Detailed tables are not in such form as to enable the public to determine the department's efficiency, nor do they give information to the public which would help locate the sources and tendencies of crime
    d No information is given in the report on administration or condition of the pension fund

Fire Department

77. The state fire marshal, the building bureau and the fire department should agree on a definite program of fire prevention
78. Members of the uniformed force may be used in making house to house inspection as in Philadelphia and Cincinnati. The inspection, conducted in certain parts of the city during May and June and resulting in a 25% to 50% reduction in fires for those months below 1912 should be continued

79. Since the police have power to enforce all ordinances, fire department orders might be countersigned by the chief of police

80. For all large establishments, sketches of internal arrangements, etc., should be prepared for the general use of the department

81. The department should conduct an educational campaign for fire prevention, similar to that conducted for disease prevention by the health department

82. Maps showing district of company, buildings in which combustibles are stored, etc., should be provided for each station house

83. Each company should be provided with a list of the buildings in its first alarm area, which are equipped with standpipes and sprinklers

84. As in the case of candidates to the police force, fire department candidates are not medically examined until they have passed written examinations. A medical test should be made when the application is first received

85. Promotion is based entirely on written examination. Promotion should be based in part on a careful record of service performed

86. Records of service efficiency should be kept

Health Department

87. Sanitary inspectors, who are not physicians, are not suitably equipped to make inspections of contagious diseases and to point out ways of avoiding contagion. This work should be transferred to visiting nurses

88. Control over contagious cases is modified by a rule which exempts the householder, in whose home a contagious disease occurs, from the daily visit of the inspectors, provided he will in writing discharge the department from responsibility

89. It is suggested that educational work be extended to this division and that nurses be assigned to instruct parents in prophylactic methods

90. Supervision should be exercised over return of children to school
91. There is no compulsory vaccination
92. The health department should encourage the use of serums for the control of disease, by distributing them liberally
93. There should be systematic health supervision of children in parochial schools
94. A resident physician should be stationed at the isolation hospital and the matron relieved of full responsibility for medical attention
95. Completeness of birth reports should be checked
96. The large number of slaughter houses makes thorough inspection of meat by present staff impossible. The chief food inspector suggests the establishment of a municipal slaughter house
97. State law does not require railroads to provide refrigerator cars for milk. During the summer months these cars are necessary to protect milk being shipped
98. Bacteriological tests are practically limited to July and August. This is undesirable. They should be made throughout the year, to prevent carelessness on the part of dealers
99. Periodical publicity should be given to all milk tests and reports should state dealers' names, etc.
100. No grades of milk have been established. There should be different grades of milk for infant feeding and for cooking purposes
101. The work of nurses who visit infants would be greatly facilitated, if it were more extensively advertised
102. An effective advertisement would be to supply, at cost, milk for infants or for nursing mothers at the baby stations
103. Attractive posters could be distributed by school children, and greater publicity of the location of baby welfare stations could be obtained through the press
104. Complainants should be informed of action taken on their complaints

105. Attention should be given to housing conditions, especially in the neighborhood of two of the baby welfare stations specially examined in this survey
106. Tenements should be subjected to systematic inspection
107. Inspectors' information on housing conditions should be recorded in such manner as to make it valuable in city planning or in securing a more modern building code
108. The department should supervise the construction and alteration of buildings, in order to insure proper provision for light and air
109. Special articles in "Healthology" are sometimes not well timed. Statistical tables would be more helpful if lucidly explained in the text of the report
110. Only from nurses visiting tubercular cases are adequate reports demanded. This method of rendering daily reports should be required in all branches of the department
111. The annual report should contain operation statistical tables showing work done, action taken and results obtained

Emergency Hospital

112. Because of internal construction, etc., the emergency hospital is totally unfit for hospital purposes. A new building should be promptly provided

Park Board

113. The city should have a comprehensive park, playground and boulevard plan far in advance of present requirements
114. Accounting control should be exercised over stores and equipment
115. Accounts are kept on a cash instead of a liability basis
116. Comparative maintenance costs should be kept
117. Arc instead of naphtha lamps should be installed in parks
118. Park privileges should be advertised before they are let, so as to receive the benefit of competition

Bureau of Weights and Measures

119. More information and detail should be given in the card register
120. Tabs of different colors should be used to show whether violations are due to carelessness or fraud
121. Condemnation tags should bear the seal of the city and should be printed in foreign languages for the foreign population
122. Seal tags should be numbered serially and a record made of number used
123. The dealer's report form should provide for schedule of weights used
124. Inspectors' report slips should provide for certification
125. The annual report does not do justice to the work of the bureau
126. The tables contained in the report should show degree of inaccuracy or dishonesty of weights and measures
127. The report should give information on discovered means of practicing fraud, or on number of scales and weights and measures confiscated
128. Additional statistics are suggested which would illuminate the report, such as tables of
    a Places inspected according to character of business
    b Promiscuous peddler and huckster inspection
    c Tests made of institutional and city department scales
    d Classification of apparatus and number of each type condemned
    e Apparatus confiscated and destroyed
    f Number of new scales, weights and measures sealed during the year
    g Comparing by years, the number of routine inspections as against special inspections
    h Purchases made for testing the manipulation of scales
    i Number of tests made of packing companies' products and results of such tests

j Complaints received and action taken

k Number of household weighing equipments tested on request

l Number of inspections made by each inspector or deputy by months, etc.

m Number of inspections made of public markets and violations found

n Violations where actual fraud was practiced, classified according to business and apparatus

Board of City Service Commissioners

129. The board has no way of learning whether employees are actually engaged on the work for which they were examined. Titles and actual duties should be stated on payrolls

130. The board should utilize its powers of approval to provide tests for promotion

131. Efficiency records should be prescribed and kept in all departments, and periodical ratings communicated to the board

132. The board should exercise its powers to investigate enforcement of civil service laws. It should study departmental conditions continuously in order to adjust civil service tests and standards to the practical requirements of departments

SUMMARY OF CRITICISMS AND CONSTRUCTIVE SUGGESTIONS REQUIRING THE PASSAGE OF ORDINANCES OR CHARTER REVISION

Mayor and Boards

1. In respect to administration the mayor is practically a figurehead. To be effective he should have fuller power and larger responsibility

2. Because of varying length of terms for which citizen boards and administrative officers are appointed, the mayor never obtains more than partial control over the responsible executive staff of the government. The term of all appointive officials should be made coördinate with that of the mayor, or better, **made indefinite with power in the mayor to remove on charges**

3. Milwaukee's city government presents a tangle of administrative control. Greater efficiency would result if all administrative boards were abolished and single heads of departments substituted. Executive officers would then be placed directly under the control and supervision of the mayor, and made responsible to him

4. The mayor, through publicity and power of popular recall, should be made responsible to the public for results

Council

5. The present council is cumbersome. Commission government and New York City's experience have clearly demonstrated that a small councilmanic commission elected at large is more representative of a city and is infinitely more efficient

Short Ballot and Home Rule

6. The city attorney and the treasurer should be made appointive instead of elective. The elective officers should consist of the mayor, the comptroller and members of the council not exceeding 15 in number

7. Milwaukee should have power to determine for itself the details of its administrative organization and procedure. At present it must look to state legislative authority for power to correct administrative defects

Charter and Administrative Code

8. A new charter is needed which will deal only with general organization and powers, and provide the following essentials:

a Minimum number of elective officials
b Maximum of centralization of responsibility
c Adequacy of popular control
d Recognized business standards
e Simplification of legislative branch

9. The details of departmental organization and a definite prescription of administrative procedure should be incorporated in *an administrative code* adopted as an ordinance and subject to local amendment after due publicity and discussion

Assessment and Collection of Taxes

10. The provision that tax assessors must reside in the wards in which they make assessments is unnecessary, and is more likely to decrease the efficiency and fairness of assessments than to promote them. It is suggested that the charter be amended in this respect

11. Tax assessments are begun on May 1st and continue for two weeks. They should be begun on January 1st and continue for six months. This readjustment would result in full time employment for assessors, a reduced force, and would open the door to better service

Decentralized Financial Control

12. Due to semi-independent board organization financial control is decentralized. Special appropriations amounting to 24.18% of the 1913 budget were made to administrative boards pursuant to mandatory provisions of the charter. Special funds should be abolished, and the expenditures of these boards provided for out of the general fund

Department of Public Works

13. The charter requires the commissioner to maintain an automobile for official use. The city should provide transportation for officials

14. In determining charges for street cleaning against property benefited, " overhead " cost should be included. Legislative authority should be obtained to permit this charge

Purchasing Division

15. Purchasing is not fully centralized. The park department should utilize the services of the purchasing agent, instead of buying independently
16. A superintendent of purchases should be appointed by and placed under the control of the mayor

City Engineer

17. Division engineers, now under a special assistant engineer, should be made subordinate to the superintendent of street construction until such time as an engineering division is organized
18. The office of city engineer, now a survival, should be abolished and the position of chief engineer created
19. The chief engineer should be made subordinate to the commissioner and responsible to him for all engineering work. He should be appointed for a term coördinate with his superior. If this position were on the civil service list, it would tend to become permanent. It is highly important that there should be continuity of policy in engineering matters

Bureau of Street Construction and Repair

20. Under present laws pavement up-keep is seriously handicapped. Local property owners or ward representatives should not be consulted in determining where and when a street should be repaved. Repaving should be governed by considerations of economy of maintenance and convenience of traffic. It is unfair to charge owners of abutting property with cost of repaving. This should be made a general charge

21. A special division or bureau of pavement maintenance should be established and all construction work placed under the superintendent of street construction
22. Park roads should be placed under the care of the bureau of street construction and repair
23. Contractors are paid by certificate for improvements assessable against owners of abutting property and not directly out of the city treasury. By using the city's instead of the contractor's credit, property owners would receive the benefit of the city's ability to borrow at lower rates of interest
24. Streets and sidewalks should be kept free from encumbrances. If necessary, special inspectors should be provided for this purpose

Bureau of Sanitation

25. The present ward organization is a survival. Steps should be taken at once scientifically to re-district the city for the work of street cleaning. The mere fact that the work is sub-divided by wards furnishes a continuing inducement to political interference
26. Laborers do not receive their wages with suitable promptness. This is due, it is stated, to delay caused by the unnecessary but legally required approval of payrolls by aldermen
27. Control over household garbage receptacles should be transferred from the health department to the bureau of sanitation

Department of Bridges and Public Buildings

28. A repair squad should be organized to make all current repairs to bridges and to all city buildings
29. All building construction, including schools and park buildings, should be centralized in this bureau

Police Department

30. The present system of instruction for recruits does not fulfill the requirements of modern police training
31. Recruits, before admission to active duty, should be placed in a recruit school for full time for 30 to 90 days. A carefully planned scheme of instruction should be established and competent instructors employed
32. The school should conduct courses in the most advanced police methods for all members of the force
33. The ten hour patrol should be discontinued, as it entails hardship on the patrolman and minimizes his efficiency
34. There are no mounted patrolmen. Mounted patrolmen are very useful and should be employed
35. It is suggested that trained police dogs be used as aids to patrolmen in outlying districts
36. Punishment by assignment to laborious duty, revocation of days off, etc., should be substituted for punishment by fines
37. The pension fund is inadequate for the needs of the department. A study should be made of the average length of service of former members of the force in order that an *actuarial* basis may be established, instead of the present method
38. The city should immediately appropriate a sum sufficient to improve the sanitary condition of the central station house, and to replace the cell house at station No. 3, which is unfit for use. There is great need of additional station houses
39. Additional police matrons should be appointed

Fire Department

40. The results of systematic intensive inspection of buildings recently conducted in the fourth ward during the disturbance of pavements showed conclusively the benefits of vigorous fire prevention work. The methods employed for this special occasion should be adopted as the general practice of the department

41. The fire department should employ a licensed physician as a regular member of its staff
42. Milwaukee is backward in regard to fire-prevention laws and ordinances. The fire chief should have power to enforce preventive measures as broad as those recently granted the fire commissioner in New York City
43. The purchase of horses should be discontinued and the installation of motor fire-fighting apparatus extended

Health Department

44. More adequate financial support is needed for health work
45. A health board should be established with power to frame and adopt a sanitary code and special health regulations
46. The department should employ at least five physicians at full time
47. Free medical service should be provided for children of indigent parents
48. In respect of tuberculosis cases it would be desirable to give the health department the power of forcible removal to the hospital
49. A city tuberculosis clinic should be established
50. Midwives should be subjected to regular inspection and should be instructed in hygienic practices
51. Funds should be provided to enable the department to control effectively the *sources* of the milk supply. Farm inspection should be extended
52. The department should seek the coöperation of the department of public works in eliminating privy vaults as rapidly as possible

Park Board

53. The board should be abolished and the department placed under a single head responsible to the mayor
54. Building and maintenance of park roads should be transferred to the bureau of street construction and repair

55. The park police should be consolidated with the general police and placed under the supervision of the police chief

56. Supplies for the department should be bought by the central purchasing division in the department of public works instead of independently. An analysis should be made of supplies regularly required and contracts executed on the basis of this analysis

57. Street trees should be placed under the care of the park department, and, if necessary, cared for out of general city funds

58. The department should request the health department to inspect all food stuffs sold in the parks

Bureau of Weights and Measures

59. The new ordinance passed in 1909 does not give the sealer powers necessary for effective work. The following additions are suggested:

    a The sealer should be empowered to condemn and destroy outright apparatus beyond repair or deliberately falsified

    b A penalty of $25 should be imposed for unauthorized removal of a "condemned" tag

    c The sealer should have specifically conferred upon him power to exclude undesirable types of weights and measures

    d The ordinance should require owners of scales to display conspicuously certificates of inspection

    e The sealer should be given power to revoke licenses of peddlers convicted of short-weighing or short-measuring

Board of City Service Commissioners

60. The practice of frequent removals of the clerical and technical forces nullifies the advantage of the merit system. All employees should be given notice of intended removal and afforded an opportunity to be heard

61. The board should be required to examine and select all city employees. Policemen and firemen are now independently examined by the police and fire board

62. Selection of appointees should be made in the order of their standing, and appointing officers should not be permitted to juggle with the civil service lists

63. Rule XVIII permits the transfer of laborers who receive no examination to the class appointed after examination. This rule gives the board power to circumvent the civil service law, and should be abolished

64. Standards for laborers are too low. Foremen are given too much latitude in determining fitness of laborers assigned to them

SUMMARY OF SUGGESTED NEXT STEPS FOR INCREASING THE EFFICIENCY OF MILWAUKEE'S CITY GOVERNMENT

1. It is recommended that there be established a competently organized Citizens' Bureau of Municipal Efficiency, equipped to coöperate effectively with experts inside the city government, and to conduct day by day a publicity, educational campaign

2. A Citizens' Bureau should:

   a Provide expert assistance to the deputy comptroller in reviewing, formulating and installing a uniform system of accounts

   b Organize public interest in the preparation of the annual city budget, and coöperate with the board of estimate in analyzing departmental requests

   c Inaugurate plans for charter revision

   d Coöperate in public works betterment

   e Help in formulating a city plan

   f Make a coöperative city-wide health study

   g Within limitation of funds available, coöperate with the bureau of municipal research in making a comprehensive detailed study of the administration of every department

33

MILWAUKEE

Incorporated in 1846, Milwaukee is the twelfth city in the United States in respect of population. The assessed valuation of its taxable property was in 1912 $460,548,763. In point of annual expenditures, Milwaukee stands sixteenth among American cities, its budget for 1913 totaling $7,866,916.03. Its outstanding bonded indebtedness is $10,046,750, less than 2.2% of the assessed value of the city's taxable realty. In industrial activity Milwaukee is in the front rank of American municipalities. Its population is in a large degree homogeneous, 225,000 being of German extraction.

Milwaukee's government consists of 41 elective officials, including a mayor, comptroller, city treasurer, city attorney, school board, judges, and a common council of 37 members, 25 elected to represent the 25 wards of the city, and 12 members elected at large. The city government is subdivided into 24 boards and administrative departments.

The metropolis of the state of Wisconsin, Milwaukee is the only city of the first class in the legislative classification of the cities of that state. It is governed in large measure by the state legislature, having practically no home rule powers.

Its present charter was granted in 1874. Since that time with each biennial session of the legislature, additions and amendments have been made, until now the instrument is a puzzle for lawyers and a hopeless tangle for the average citizen.

PART ONE

RESPONSIBLE GOVERNMENT OF THE CITY

Mayor's Powers Too Limited

Undoubtedly, Milwaukee citizens generally regard the mayor as responsible for the character of government the city receives. Yet the mayor in Milwaukee in his own words, " is practically a figurehead ". Milwaukee is without a chief executive charged with responsibility for carrying out a definite program of administration and armed with power to execute such a program. The mayor to be effective should have fuller power and larger responsibility.

The Mayor an Observer

In an administrative sense the mayor is, to a large degree, merely an observer of what transpires in city government, with power, through his conspicuous position, to create public sentiment. As an observer he is effective only as he is informed of occurrences.

" The Mayor's Eye "

Finding that he has literally no means of controlling the departments of the city except as he is able through special inquiry to obtain information to influence their conduct, the present mayor brought about on January 1, 1913, the establishment of a bureau of municipal research as a part of his own office organization. This bureau is the mayor's " official eye ". The director of the bureau is under the supervision of the mayor and comptroller, and is authorized by ordinance to make inquiries into the administration of the several offices of the city government. The powers granted the bureau represent all the effective administrative power that the mayor of the city possesses as the head of the government. The establishment of an agency of information as a part of the organization of the mayor's office was a step of the utmost importance in promoting the effectiveness of the mayoralty. Through the bureau the mayor is able to suggest to the council or department heads means of improving administrative methods, and with the comptroller's consent, to investigate conditions which in his judgment need attention.

Divided and Decentralized Responsibility Pictured

The accompanying chart pictures the organization of the city with special reference to the location of responsibility. As the chart shows, the elective officials responsible to the people consist of a mayor, treasurer, comptroller, a board of school directors, judges of the municipal courts elected for terms of two years, and a common council with two and four year terms. Of these, only the mayor and the council and in a smaller degree, the comptroller, are held responsible by the electorate for the scope and character of service rendered by the general administrative departments of the city.

In the chart the appointive administratve officials and boards are represented by the row of small oblongs at the base, and consist of the following:

BOARDS

Name	Number Members	Appointed by	Term
Public land commissioners	5 citizens	Mayor, confirmed by council	5 yrs., 1 ea. yr.
Fire and police board	5 citizens	Mayor	5 yrs., 1 ea. yr.
Park board	5 citizens	Mayor, confirmed by council	5 yrs., 1 ea. yr.
City service commissioners	4 citizens	Mayor	4 yrs., 1 ea. yr.
Public museum	4 citizens	Mayor	4 yrs., 1 ea. yr.
	3 aldermen	Mayor	2 years
	2 ex-officio: pres. school bd. supt. of schools	—	
Public library	4 citizens	Public library bd.	4 yrs., 1 ea. yr.
	3 aldermen	Mayor	2 yrs.
	2 ex-officio: pres. school bd. supt. of schools	—	—
Art commission	4 citizens	Ex-officio members	4 yrs., 1 ea. yr.
	3 ex-officio: pres. park board pres. pub. mus. bd. pres. school bd.	—	—
Public debt commission	3 citizens	Mayor, confirmed by council	3 yrs., 1 ea. yr.
Harbor commission	9 citizens	Mayor, confirmed by council	3 yrs., 3 ea. yr.
	5 aldermen	Mayor, confirmed by council	3 yrs.
	1 ex-officio: com. pub. wks.	—	—
Emergency hospital	5 physicians	Mayor	2 yrs.
	3 aldermen	Mayor	2 yrs.
	1 ex-officio: health com.	—	—

CHART SHOWING ORGANIZATION OF MILWAUKEE'S CITY GOVERNMENT

NEW YO

PUL

V

Director *P*

Deputy *C*

Third Assis

Librarian

Draughts m

Name	Number Members	Appointed by	Term
Local board of industrial education	4 citizens 1 ex-officio: supt. schools	Board school directors —	2 yrs., 2 ea. yr. —
Building code commission	10 citizens 3 aldermen 3 ex-officio: insp. of bldgs. city engineer chief fire dept.	Council Council —	Until code is complete " " " " —
Free employment bureau	5 citizens 5 citizens 5 citizens 5 citizens	Mchts. & Mfgs. Ass'n. County bd. supervisors Federated Trades Co. Pres. of council	Indefinite " " "
Examiner of stationary engineers	2 examiners	Mayor	During good behavior

ADMINISTRATIVE OFFICIALS

Name	Appointed by				Term
Smoke inspector	Mayor, confirmed by council				4 years
Inspector of buildings	"	"	"	"	4 years
Commissioner of public health	"	"	"	"	4 years
City engineer	"	"	"	'	3 years
Water registrar	"	"	"	"	3 years
Tax commissioner	"	"	"	"	3 years
Commissioner public works	"	"	"	"	2 years
Director, bureau of municipal research	"	"	"	"	2 years
City clerk	Council,				2 years
Sealer of weights and measures	Mayor,	"	"	"	Indefinite

Mayor Appoints with Approval of Council

With one or two minor exceptions where appointments are made by the council or its president, the mayor appoints all single heads of departments and all members of boards except those serving ex-officio or appointed by ex-officio members. With six exceptions these appointments are made with the approval of the council.

Mayor Never Obtains Complete Control

Because of the varying length of the terms of board members and administrative officers no mayor ever obtains complete control over the responsible executive staff of the government. The public library, park, fire and police boards are never under the control of the mayor, for consisting of five members appointed serially, one each year, at least three are always hold-over appointees. Mayors who have passed out of office have more responsibility for the conduct of these departments than the mayor in power.

The mayor's term is two years, but the health commissioner, the inspector of buildings and the smoke inspector whom he appoints have terms twice as long. For no apparent reason at all, other important administrative officials, such as the city engineer and the tax commissioner, have three year terms, though they are appointed by a mayor with a term of two. An incoming mayor either finds these vitally important offices filled for his entire term, or is called upon to fill them when his term is half over, chiefly for the benefit or embarrassment of his successor, or appoints them at the beginning of his term for double or half again the period of his own tenure.

Besides the director of the bureau of municipal research the only administrative officer whose term begins and ends with the mayor's is the commissioner of public works. The commissioner, it is true, is the most important administrative official of the city government, but even he is not wholly under the control of the mayor. The council must approve his appointment and only the council has power to remove him. Except in so far as he can exercise control through the power of inquiry held by the bureau of municipal research, the mayor has only a *persuasive* influence over the activities of the commissioner of public works.

There is no uniformity nor virtue in all this, merely a somewhat interesting variety. Political appointments are often easier to make when a term is half expired and the public is unconcerned, than when the public is on tip-toe to learn from the character of appointments the kind of administration that an incoming mayor is likely to give.

Mayor Should Control Appointive Officials

The term of all appointive officials should be made coördinate with that of the mayor, or better, made indefinite with power in the mayor to remove on charges after a hearing. So long as a mayor is elected and the formulation of a city program is made an incident of his election, the mayor, subject to proper control, should be given power to carry out that program. This means that the mayor should be regarded as the general manager of the city with power to direct the subordinate administrative officers of the government.

City Government a Tangle of Administrative Control

Milwaukee's city government has been developed through a process of accretion. Department after department, office after office, has been added by state legislation or ordinance. Each successive addition has been made without reference to the kind of organization prescribed for boards or departments earlier established. The result is that as now constituted the city government contains the greatest diversity of forms of organization and presents a tangle of administrative control.

It is inconceivable that any one organizing the government of the city of Milwaukee with a view to obtaining efficient results would organize it as now constituted. Each addition to the varied structure of the government seems to have been a compromise between a public desire or need for extension of service, and a fear of its subversion to some political misuse.

Citizen Administrative Boards

To place a citizen board, such as the police and fire or park boards, at the head of an administrative department is not peculiar to Milwaukee. But in other cities this form of organization is rapidly being discarded with the growing elimination of corrupt politics from city government. Members of citizen boards are in a majority of cases merely the recording instruments of an appointive subordinate executive actually in charge of the administration of the department over which they preside. Rarely, if ever, do citizen board members actively participate in the management of the department for which they are responsible. Indeed, it is not expected that they shall do so.

It is believed that Milwaukee would obtain results of greater efficiency if it abolished all administrative boards and followed for all departments the precedent established when a single commissioner of public works was substituted for the public works board. Executive officers would then be placed directly under the control and supervision of the mayor and made directly responsible to him for results obtained. The mayor, in turn, through systematic publicity of facts regarding city business, and the power of the popular recall, should be made responsible to the public for results.

Decentralized Financial Control

As a by-product of the semi-independent board organization there is lack of centralized control over the finances of the city. Thus, while the common council is required by the charter to frame a budget and to determine the tax rate, in respect of the school board, the board of industrial education, the public library board, city service board, board of art commissioners, park board and public museum board, it is obliged by specific charter provisions to include, within the limits of a maximum allowance authorized by the charter, such sums as these several boards estimate that they may require. Once they receive their funds these independent boards have practically complete discretion over their expenditure. In the budget for 1913, 24.18% of the total appropriations were made to these quasi-independent boards pursuant to mandatory provisions of this character.

Collection of Little Governments

Thus, not only in point of responsibility, but also in point of financial control, Milwaukee is not one city government but a collection of little city governments, each exercising a more or less irresponsible sway in its own jurisdiction.

Popular rule over Milwaukee's city government is so diluted that in regard to many of the more important functions of the municipality it is practically non-existent.

A Smaller Council

Milwaukee maintains a cumbersome elective council of 37 members. A common council of this size inevitably devotes a considerable portion of its time to more or less inconsequential debate, because the atmosphere created is that of a " deliberative " assemblage rather than a board of business directors such as the council of a municipality should be. Commission government has clearly demonstrated that a small councilmanic commission elected at large is wholly competent to deal with the legislative problems of a municipality. The experience of New York City has shown conclusively that a board of estimate and apportionment consisting of eight officials either elected at large or by boroughs, is beyond question more efficient, and generally more representative of the city, than a board of aldermen elected by wards. The council now performs certain administrative functions, such as approval of vouchers and payrolls, that proper budget making and effective auditing by the comptroller would render unnecessary. A proposed charter amendment* discontinues the councilmanic audit of bills.

Short Ballot

The city attorney and the treasurer are now chosen by the electorate. A city attorney must, in large measure, serve as the legal adviser of the mayor and department heads. He should therefore be in sympathy with the program of the administration in power. Unless it is assumed that the mayor will utilize his office for political rather than administrative ends, the city attorney should be appointed by the mayor and subject to removal by him.

The city treasurer exercises no discretionary powers. Under modern methods of protection through bonding and auditing, there is no reason for encumbering a ballot with the names of candidates for city treasurer. The mayor, if competent to conduct the affairs of the city government, is surely competent to appoint a city treasurer.

The elective officers should consist of the mayor, the comptroller and members of the council, the latter not exceeding fifteen in number.

---

* To become law June, 1913.

Home Rule for Milwaukee

Milwaukee should be able to determine for itself the details of its administrative organization and procedure. Under present conditions the city is compelled to resort to the state legislature for power to conform to reasonable business standards in the administration of its affairs. The legislature meets biennially. Therefore, in the intervening period the city is wholly without power to correct defects in existing administrative provisions or make desired additions, often of the most important character. It is everywhere recognized as futile to attempt to regulate the administrative details of a great municipality, such as Milwaukee, through state legislation.

Milwaukee Needs a New Charter

It would seem entirely feasible to frame a charter for Milwaukee which would be comprised within a few pages, and which, because it dealt only with general organization and powers, might be kept unchanged indefinitely.

The details of departmental organization and procedure should be incorporated in an administrative code adopted as an ordinance and subject to local amendment after due publicity and discussion.

Citizens of Milwaukee desiring to establish efficient city government should seek to obtain a charter for Milwaukee which would provide the following essentials:

1. Minimum number of elective officials
2. Maximum of centralization of responsibility
3. Adequacy of popular control through publicity and power to recall elective officials
4. Recognized business standards in respect of such items as accounting, reporting, budget making, letting of contracts, making purchases, civil service and salary standardization
5. Definite prescription of administrative procedure
6. Simplification of the legislative branch through reduction in size

PART TWO

ADMINISTRATION OF THE CITY

Milwaukee Well Started Towards Administrative Efficiency

Despite charter complexity and scattered responsibility, Milwaukee has a government abreast of the most progressive cities of the country in scope of activity and above the average in administrative method. Such important activities as health work, weights and measures control and public works have received intelligent attention. Moreover, there are not to be found the customary crudities of business method in accounting, budget making and purchasing. These processes, though by no means on a completely efficient basis, have already evolved out of the customary rule-of-thumb stage and are now undergoing further improvement.

MAYOR'S OFFICE

Activities of the Mayor's Research Bureau

A notable fact to be recorded in respect of the mayor's office is the recent establishment of the bureau of municipal research. This bureau will not only help the mayor vitalize his leadership in constructive improvements of city government, but will serve as a point of contact between the mayor's office and the proposed Milwaukee Citizens' Bureau of Municipal Efficiency.

The mayor's bureau of municipal research, as now constituted, has taken the place of the bureau of economy and efficiency, conducted during the previous administration as the efficiency agent of the city government.

According to the statement of its director, the bureau of municipal research since the beginning of the year, has:

1. "Rearranged the 1913 budget, functionalized it, and classified expenditures previous to its adoption, January 31st
2. "Entered upon the work of standardizing salaries, and the writing of individual cards for every city position
3. "Conducted several investigations not yet made public, one being the analysis of the 1912 purchases by the purchasing department, still under way
4. "Coöperated with the city attorney's office and city departments in drafting charter legislation in relation to:

43

(a), change in budget procedure; (b), adoption of 'lot and block' system in taxing property; (c), increasing powers of the comptroller: authorizing him to standardize payrolls, to prescribe methods of accounting in city departments, and to discontinue present red tape of sending vouchers to common council for approval; (d), improvement in organization of water department—elimination of water registrar and deputy; (e), collection of taxes twice a year; (f), permitting payment for local assessment when work is completed."

Its plans for prospective work include:

1. " Salary standardization
2. " Coöperation with civil service board to reorganize civil service procedure
3. " Drafting of forms and budget procedure (departmental detailed requests and examiners' analyses) for fall preparation of budget "

The bureau's coöperation with other city departments has already resulted in notable improvement in the form of the city budget. On its initiative the state legislature has recently passed several important bills affecting budget making, accounting and salary revision.

The time is peculiarly ripe and the opportunity most favorable for vigorous constructive coöperation between officials and citizens. If a definite program is adopted and efficient service supplied it should be possible to establish, before the conclusion of the present administration, standards of efficiency which will help or compel succeeding administrations to render increasingly adequate service.

Additional Opportunities for Leadership Suggested

It is suggested that the mayor invite the members of the various boards and departments to meet with him periodically in order to discuss and adopt a common administrative program. Specifically, it is suggested that the mayor attempt to obtain the agreement of the park, police and fire, education and other boards and departments, to some such program as the following, nearly all of which can be put into effect without legislation:

1. Use by all the departments of the city government of the central purchasing division for the purchase of all supplies

2. Immediate institution in all city departments of a uniform system of accounts as prescribed by the comptroller. Recent legislation, it is true, gives the comptroller power to prescribe accounts and a uniform payroll procedure for all departments. But the experience of other cities proves that prescription is not enough. The installation and operation of new accounts require the coöperation of the clerical force of all departments. The mayor, as the head of the city government, by helping all departments recognize the importance of proper accounting and obtaining their agreement to a common program, can greatly facilitate the execution of the comptroller's plans

3. Regular submission to the mayor by all departments of reports showing the significant facts of operation and expenditure

4. Uniform working hours: minimum, 9 A. M. to 5 P. M., or 8.30 A. M. to 5 P. M. throughout the year, except Saturdays

5. Time reports for all clerical forces and subordinate administrative officials, as well as foremen and laborers

6. A uniform system of expense, stores and cost accounts wherever cost accounts are applicable, as planned by the comptroller

7. Adoption of uniform rules and regulations with regard to office practice

8. Standardization of departmental reports to eliminate waste through verbiage, meaningless schedules, etc., and to insure prompt submission and publication

9. Standardization of salaries, in order that employees performing similar work in different departments may receive like compensation, due allowance being made for experience and length of service

10. Centralized civil service control over all departments, particularly in regard to the holding of examinations (requires legislation)

11. Establishment of uniform efficiency records in coöperation with the city service commission

12. Establishment of a uniform system of promotion based upon efficiency of service and promotional examinations

13. Standardization of office equipment, filing systems, etc.

14. Holding departmental conferences and conducting educational courses for the clerical service, engineers and engineering corps, police and firemen, with a view to in-

creasing the efficiency of city employees and facilitating their promotion

15. Centralizing services where such centralization is feasible, as, for example, transferring to the public works department responsibility for maintaining park roads, establishment of a central repair department for repairing all equipment and buildings, including schools, libraries, etc.

16. Establishing a central bureau of information, complaints and publicity, to be used by all departments and by citizens complaining or inquiring concerning the work of any department

These and other steps which will be suggested in subsequent pages of this report may be taken by the city government with little change in the existing laws and no additional expenditure, provided the mayor is able to obtain the voluntary coöperation of the several administrative boards of the city. Many of these proposed steps will mean greater economy. All will mean increased efficiency. None of the steps suggested would mean the forfeiture or relinquishment of any power now exercised by these boards. If repairs to park roads were turned over to the public works department, it would mean merely that the public works department would make these repairs as the agent of the park board and subject to its general supervision. If all supplies were purchased by the central purchasing agent instead of as now, independently, by the secretary of the park board, the purchasing agent of the board of education, etc., it would still be possible for those boards to control their funds while obtaining the advantages of economy that must result when purchases are made by an efficient central agency.

By accepting the full obligations of his office and making it, through the bureau of municipal research, the business standardizing department of the city government, the present mayor has taken an effective step towards obtaining a re-definition of the mayor's powers. With his present program continued and developed public reliance on the mayoralty will be increased and the futility clearly shown of employing a man to take leadership in the management of the city and then curbing his power in every conceivable way.

COMPTROLLER

Accounting Improvement Needed and Begun

Though considerable attention has been given to the accounts and records of the city, accounting methods are as yet by no means adequately standardized in the city departments, nor has a complete modern system been installed in the comptroller's office itself. Responsibility for the accounts of the city seems by custom to be committed to the deputy comptroller.

Comptroller's Plans Approved

The deputy comptroller, under the supervision of the comptroller, has outlined an adequate system to be installed in the comptroller's office, which will include (1) a general ledger; (2) a property ledger; (3) appropriation ledgers; (4) subsidiary registers for listing resolutions, contracts, orders, vouchers and warrants to be used as posting mediums to the appropriation ledgers and to the general ledger accounts.

In addition, the deputy comptroller plans for all departments a uniform system of payrolls, vouchers, registers, appropriation ledgers, stores ledgers, etc. Expense ledgers to show distribution of expenditures by function and purpose of expenditure will also be installed, as well as unit cost records, for all activities which are measurable by significant units.

Present Methods Soon To Be Superseded

The accounting expert of this Bureau sent to Milwaukee to study the accounting needs of the city was requested by the deputy comptroller and the director of the bureau of municipal research to devote his time to consultation on the proposed new installation. Inasmuch as the responsible officer seems to have a clear understanding of existing accounting defects and a definite plan for correcting them, this request was complied with and only a cursory review made of present methods. These methods will be supplanted with approved practices as fast as their installation can be made.

It must not be understood that the accounts are at present up to the best standards of efficiency. On the contrary there are many conditions requiring attention not only in the comptroller's office but throughout the departments. But this fact is thoroughly appreciated by the deputy comptroller.

So important to good administration are efficient accounting practices that it is earnestly hoped that the administration as a whole will coöperate in carrying into effect the present excellent plans of the comptroller's office to place the accounting of the city on an efficient and scientific basis. If the installation as now planned is successfully completed at the conclusion of the present term, Milwaukee will have very genuine cause for congratulation.

Charter Defect Corrected

The charter of Milwaukee does not recognize the necessity for vesting in a central officer responsibility for the accounting processes of the city. This defect, common to many American charters, has been remedied by a bill introduced at the present legislature at the suggestion of the city authorities. This measure gives adequate power to the comptroller to prescribe for every department of the city a modern and, as far as practicable, a uniform system of accounts.

Comptroller as Auditor

The chief function of the comptroller is to audit claims against the city and payments due the city, in order that no funds may be paid except for value received, and that all money due the city may be properly collected. There are numerous important defects in the present auditing practice, all of which are recognized by the deputy comptroller, who plans to correct them. The following are cited merely by way of illustration:

1. All payments on account of contracts are checked by the comptroller as to accuracy, but no provision is made for comparing the certificates of payment with the terms of contract or specifications. Files of contracts are not kept in the comptroller's office, and only a brief description of contract terms is transcribed on the comptroller's records. A complete contract file should be maintained in the comptroller's office and all contract payments carefully compared with contract provisions

2. For the audit of payrolls a card record is kept of appointments approved by the city service commission. This

record, however, is based on a similar record kept in the commission's office, whose accuracy the comptroller does not verify

3. Several of the departments do not keep time records to support their payrolls. Consequently, the comptroller is obliged to place full responsibility on the approval of the department heads for accuracy of claims for service rendered. Even these approvals are rarely in the form of a legally binding certificate. Payroll preparation and certificates are in urgent need of revision. Payrolls should be based on time reports certified by the employee himself or by his foreman. All payrolls should bear a certificate to the effect that they are based on time reports properly certified. Payrolls should be certified by the person who prepares them and who has the records of service before him, as well as by the head of the bureau or department

4. Central control has not been established over financial stationery, such as licenses, permits, etc., and only in respect of a limited number of revenues, such as those derived from permits, are reports received which furnish a basis for a check on the treasurer

5. Over so important a matter as the collection of taxes, control is exercised only through the total amount of the tax roll. Tax bills should be made in multiple copies and a copy filed with the comptroller as a basis for auditing all collections

6. As yet the comptroller has conducted no audit of departmental accounts, although he is authorized to do so. His deputy informed us that such audits are now definitely contemplated

Scope of Reform Provided by New Act

In addition to betterment of accounting methods, the recent act enlarging the comptroller's power permits other important improvements, as for example:

1. Discontinuance of useless practice of submitting all claims to council before payment and subsequent printing in the proceedings of council

2. Prescription of uniform payrolls and requirement that the person who prepares the payroll and has knowledge of the facts certify to its correctness

3. Making available to public inspection and audit "at all times" all warrants drawn by the city

4. Giving the comptroller power to investigate the records of all officers, boards and departments and to prescribe forms of reports

These additions to the power of the city's chief business officer are of the greatest importance. If effectively used they will increase the efficiency of every branch of the city government.

TAX COMMISSIONER

Ward Lines and Assessments

In the assessment of taxes, as in the case of local improvements, the treatment of the city as a collection of political units, is required, for tax assessors must be residents of the wards in which they make assessments. This requirement is probably a survival of the time when separate tax rates were established for the several wards and separate ward funds maintained. The mere fact that an appraiser resides within a ward of a large city is not likely to give him any special qualification for assessing the property of that ward. The provision is unnecessary and is more likely to decrease the efficiency and fairness of assessments than to promote them.

Excellent Features in Taxing Methods

There are many excellent features in taxing methods in use in Milwaukee. Particularly praiseworthy is the practice of assessing real property at full value. Full value assessments were inaugurated in 1911, when valuations were increased from $247,-573,150 in 1910 to $442,932,255. This will reduce the chance of discrimination which exists when partial value assessments are made. Other noteworthy features are the separate assessments of land and improvements and the assessment of vacant land at market value. Frequently in other cities discrimination is made in favor of owners of vacant land.

Under a recent act of legislature, the " lot and block " system of describing property for purposes of taxation is to be adopted in Milwaukee. Heretofore, property has been described by location and ownership. The " lot and block " system facilitates identification of particular parcels and reduces the opportunity for error in billing taxes or special assessments.

Full Time Assessors

Taxes are assessed as of May 1st and assessments are made during May and June. During a large part of the year assessors are idle. Assessments should be made as of January 1st and the work of assessing begun on that date. This change is advocated by the present tax commissioner who states that year-round work would permit of a considerable reduction in the number of assessors. This change would, of course, require a legislative act.

BUDGET MAKING

Budget Improvement

The first requirements of good budget making are clarity of authorization and definiteness of limitation upon expenditure. Within the limits of the then existing law the present Milwaukee budget, adopted in January, 1913, conforms to the new standards of budget making recently established in New York, Philadelphia, Chicago and other large cities. An act passed by the legislature at its recent session at the suggestion of the Milwaukee research bureau lays the basis for a thoroughly modern and efficient budget procedure.

Legal Obstacles Removed and Good Practice Provided

Prior to the passage of this act the budget was voted on January 31st, although the fiscal year began January 1st. For the first month of the year, therefore, the departments spent money not yet appropriated, and the city was without a definite financial program. Under the new act the budget will be voted on December 31st, to take effect with the beginning of the fiscal year.

Prior to the passage of the new budget law, before the budget could be adopted by council, estimates for appropriations were reviewed first by a board of estimate and subsequently by the finance committee of the council. Under the new law, the finance committee is made a part of the board of estimate, and separate action by it is no longer required. By combining the finance committee and the board of estimate in a single body, the time consumed in budget discussion will be greatly shortened.

Prior to the passage of the new law double appropriation was required before funds became available for departmental expenditure. A first appropriation was made at the time of the passage of the budget, and a second appropriation when the departments desired to avail themselves of funds allowed them. Under the new act the adoption of the budget authorizes the departments to spend the funds provided for them, thus enabling them to plan their work with greater intelligence.

In addition to the changes in budget procedure, the new budget law requires all departments to submit uniform estimates showing in detail the necessary purposes for which the funds requested are to be spent. These estimates will be carefully reviewed by the comptroller before they are passed upon by the board of estimate and apportionment. Department heads will attend the deliberations of the board of estimate and apportionment to explain the purposes of their respective requests.

· The new law requires that at least one public hearing be given by the board of estimate before the budget is finally adopted. Under the present procedure the public is given no opportunity to participate in the preparation of the city's annual service expenditure program.

Heretofore, appropriations once made could not be changed even by action of the council. The new law permits the board of estimate at any time throughout the year to adjust appropriations within the total departmental allowances. This power enables the budget makers to vote the budget in greater detail, thus exercising fuller control over the expenditure of public funds. Because an appropriation once made was unalterable, the budget heretofore necessarily contained many appropriations whose titles did not indicate their specific purposes. Lump sum appropriations of this character are continuing inducements to ill-considered expenditure.

The power to revise is also the power to control, for the board of estimate in passing upon requests for transfers of appropriations may demand a public explanation of the reasons for changes in departmental plans.

Good Budget Making Depends on Right Accounting

Intimately related to proper budget making are the accounting records kept by the several departments. Unless these records show the amount of money spent for each of the important activities conducted by the department it is impossible to prepare honest estimates of requirements. The comptroller's plans for establishing classified expense accounts in the several departments, therefore, are essentially a part of the broader program now under way for making the preparation of the annual budget a time of reviewing publicly the accomplishments and needs of every branch of the city government. At present the accounts kept by departments are practically of no value in preparing adequate budget estimates.

The new law will enable the board of estimate and the council to prepare a budget expressing a specific, detailed program of activities and expenditures, clear in its instruction to city officials and understandable to the public. Next year's budget should have a summary showing total authorizations for all purposes according to departments and functions.

SALARY STANDARDIZATION

Proposed Revision of Salaries

As far as we are advised no city in the country has yet adopted a scientific plan for compensating its employees. Municipal salaries once fixed are likely to remain fixed until political influences accomplish a change. So little understanding have salary-fixing bodies of the details of departmental work that they have rarely undertaken to standardize compensation paid to employees on the basis of quality and quantity of work performed.

Salaries in Milwaukee are fixed by the common council. Heretofore, no changes in salaries could be made except at the first meeting of the council in January when the budget was under discussion. In the belief that the stress of budget making permitted unwise salary changes to slip through, the bureau of municipal research obtained the passage of a law authorizing the council to make salary adjustments at any time, within sixty days prior to December 1st when the budget is in preparation. The purpose of the change was to enable the council to consider requests for salary changes deliberately, previous to the time when the budget is presented to them for adoption.

Salaries Should Be Adjusted Only Once a Year

It is usually desirable to have salary questions considered only once a year, in order that department heads may not be under pressure from employees to seize favorable opportunities to obtain increases for them, and that the board may consider each salary in reference to the salaries of all other employees. Once a definite plan of compensation is established, the best time to consider salary adjustments is when the total program of departmental work and expenditure is under consideration. This time is the time of budget making.

In order to avoid annoyance from employees desiring increases and to prevent action in isolated cases, it is recommended that the council establish a rule that all requests for salary adjustments shall be submitted at a single time by all departments, once a year, unless it can be shown that some special emergency exists.

Again the Mayor's Bureau Has Work Under Way

The bureau of municipal research is now planning a study of comparative rates of compensation for the same classes of work now existing in different departments. On the basis of this study the council will be able to establish equal pay for equal work throughout the city and to lay the foundation for an equitable promotion system.

DEPARTMENT OF PUBLIC WORKS

Department Well Organized

The budget appropriation for 1913 for the department of public works is $2,573,079.74 or 32.6% of the amount appropri-

Wagon makers use streets for storage purposes—a village practice which should be discontinued.

ated by the city for operating purposes. In 1907 the state legislature permitted this department to abandon the cumbersome board form of organization which is still retained in a number of other departments of the city government. By an act of that year the office of public works commissioner was established and provision was made for organizing the department along functional lines. This provision is not specific, but is implied in the requirement that the commissioner of public works appoints a superintendent of sewerage, a superintendent of street construction and repair, a superintendent of street cleaning and collection and removal of ashes and garbage, and a superintendent of bridges and public buildings.

The department has been subdivided into bureaus, with functions corresponding to the titles of superintendents fixed by the charter. In addition to these bureaus there have been created (by ordinance) a bureau of harbors and rivers and a bureau of purchases. Under the present administration the bureau of purchases has been made a part of the deputy commissioner's office. The general plan of organization of the department, following, as it does, functional lines of activity, provides for an efficient distribution of duties.

In making suggestions regarding the work of the department of public works, it is not intended to suggest a present lack of efficiency, but merely to point out possible opportunities for further improvement.

The Commissioner

The salary of the commissioner is $5,000 but he is required by charter to provide and maintain an automobile for official use. This provision is a glaring illustration of the absurd detail to which the city is bound by legislative enactment.

The city should provide transportation for the officials of the department and pay the commissioner a salary proportionate to the value of his services without qualification.

Chief Clerk's Office

Bookkeeping Decentralized

As a matter of organization, a chief clerk is in charge of all the clerical work of the department. All clerks employed in the several bureaus are subject to his supervision. Subject to his review, the commissioner has delegated to the chief clerk power to hire and discharge the clerical force.

But the clerical work of the department is not wholly centralized. Each of the bureaus has one or more clerks directly responsible to the bureau superintendent. Certain clerical assistance is undoubtedly needed in the bureau offices. The bureau of sanitation, however, which occupies a room immediately adjoining the room occupied by the chief clerk, and the bureau of bridges and public buildings with offices on the next floor, have their own bookkeepers who are only nominally under the supervision of the chief clerk.

With the possible exception of the water department, all bookkeeping for the department should be done in the chief clerk's office.

Payroll Preparation

Payrolls for the several divisions of the department, except for the water department or bureau, are prepared and typewritten in the chief clerk's office. Considerable time and expense would be saved in the preparation of these payrolls if a mechanical process were used in writing them, similar to the process now employed in writing bills in the water department.

It was stated that payrolls for laborers are required to be signed by the payees and the signatures approved by the foremen prior to the actual payment of wages due. This practice itself vitiates the value of the receipt and should be discontinued. It was also stated that in many cases the foremen not only approved the receipt but actually wrote them themselves. If this is done it should, of course, be immediately discontinued.

The street railway company is permitted to open a number of blocks of pavement at one time, to the great inconvenience of traffic. Repairs to railway tracks should be made in stretches not larger than two blocks.

Departmental Accounts

With the exception of the beginning of a cost system in the bureau of street construction, and a fairly adequate system of expense accounts in the bureau of sanitation, the accounts of the department of public works present a virgin field for constructive work.

Because of the importance of public works activities, it is recommended that the deputy comptroller and the bureau of municipal research take up as promptly as possible a complete review of the public works records, in order that the various division heads, the commissioner, the mayor and the public, may have adequate information for controlling the operation of each of the important functions of the department.

Time Reports Not Certified

Ward superintendents in the bureau of sanitation and gang foremen in the other bureaus are required to report the time of members of their gangs and the character of work upon which they were engaged during the month or other period covered by the report. Except in one case, foremen when signing their reports do not certify them as correct. Foremen and ward superintendents should certify on all time reports that statements of fact contained in the reports are true. Uniform time reports should be provided for all labor forces, and all clerical and supervisory employees should be required to submit weekly or semi-monthly statements of time and service.

Work Reports Not Certified

In the division of street cleaning and garbage collection, ward superintendents are required to submit monthly reports showing, by weeks, the total number of catch basins cleaned, the number of loads of material removed from catch basins to the dumps, and by weeks, the total number of loads of ashes, rubbish and street sweepings collected and removed to the city dumps or garbage incinerator, as the case might be. These records furnish a basis for checking the efficiency of ward superintendents and determining the cost per unit of work performed. They should, therefore, be most carefully prepared. The report on ash and rubbish collection, however, makes no provision for the signature of the ward superintendent. On none of the reports is provision made for the superintendent's certificate of the accuracy of information contained in them.

Deliveries to Dumps Not Checked

All deliveries at the incinerator are carefully weighed and checked, so that as to these there are adequate means of verifying the accuracy of the ward superintendents' reports. No provision is made, however, for checking material delivered to public dumps, which includes material removed from catch basins, street sweepings, and a considerable part of the ashes and rubbish collected. A foreman is stationed at each dump who might readily report by number the wagons making deliveries. Only in this way can effective control be secured over work done by hired teams.

Careful Record Kept of Assessment Work

All the work in the bureau of sanitation (street cleaning) the cost of which is in part assessed against property benefited, such as street sprinkling, oiling, cutting of weeds, etc., is carefully reported by the ward superintendents in order that charges against property owners may be made with accuracy. The present law does not permit the inclusion of " overhead " cost (supervision, use of equipment, etc.) in determining amounts to be assessed. The city is not permitted to charge for water or the use of sprinklers in billing property owners for sprinkling, but only for the actual labor cost. If property owners are to bear the cost of this service the actual cost should be charged to them and not a part of the cost. Legislative authority should be obtained to permit proper billing of assessment charges.

Issue of Permits

Permits to plumbers, builders, or to city departments for excavating streets or placing building material upon street surfaces, are issued in the office of the chief clerk. The permit procedure is adequate, except in one particular. Permits are signed and issued to the applicant before the payment of the required fee. The permittee is supposed to take the permit obtained in the chief clerk's office to the treasurer, to pay his fee and receive the treasurer's stamp upon the permit. Policemen in controlling the excavation or incumbrance of streets are instructed not to honor any permit which lacks the treasurer's stamp. In other words, responsibility for preventing unauthorized use of the permits issued by the department rests upon the policeman. A simpler procedure, and one which would completely avoid the possibility of fraud, would be to require the applicant to file with the permit clerk a receipt from the treasurer before the permit is issued to him. If necessary for the convenience of applicants a special clerk detailed from the treasurer's office might be stationed in the chief clerk's office to receive collections.

Centralize Stenographic Service

Six stenographers are employed in the department. They are now attached to the several bureaus. It is suggested that a central stenographic bureau be organized under the supervision of the commissioner's secretary in order that stenographers may be assigned for specific work throughout the department as they are needed.

Filing

An excellent system of filing is being established in the central office. The correspondence for the entire department should be filed in one central filing division. Where files are kept in the several divisions a common system of classification and indexing, similar to that now being established in the commissioner's office, should be adopted.

Purchasing Division

In 1910 the previous administration established a central purchasing division in the public works department. This step was in conformance with sound business practice and was entirely commendable.

The present administration conducts a central purchasing office, but has abolished the position of purchasing agent and has placed in charge of purchases a clerk who is subordinate to the deputy commissioner.

Purchasing Records Not Kept Up

The preceding administration established a complete register of vendors dealing in supplies currently required by the city. It also established and maintained a quotation register, showing quotations made on the invitation of the purchasing agent.

Both these records have been permitted to lapse by the present administration, though they constitute important accessories to efficient purchasing.

The ordinance creating the bureau of supplies provides that the " superintendent of purchases shall keep himself constantly informed of all daily market quotations on all supplies which he may have occasion to purchase ". To carry out the intent of this ordinance a current price record should be maintained, in which there should be registered market quotations or quotations from bidders on supplies currently required by the city government.

In a measure, the quotation register established by the preceding administration would serve this purpose. In failing to maintain this record the purchasing clerk is not only violating good business practice but also the ordinance.

Buying Done on Open Market Order

The charter provides that " all work and the purchase of supplies or material * * * including incidental printing, when the cost thereof shall exceed two hundred dollars * * * shall be let by contract, to the lowest bidder ". In 1912, according to a list furnished by the purchasing clerk, $444,337.82 worth of supplies were bought by the purchasing clerk. Practically all these purchases were stated by the clerk to have been made by open market order. In addition to the list supplied by the purchasing clerk,

Sewer Basin Cleaning—The wagon box is supposedly water-tight to prevent the escape of foul water. Note the wet area under the wagon. An efficiency study should be made to learn whether three men are necessary to clean one basin.

the commissioner of public works informed us that materials and equipment to the amount of $186,436.55 were purchased in 1912 on contract. Of the $186,436.55 contracted for, $81,185 was for coal and $35,775 for crushed stone. The balance was for such items as telegraph cables, fire hydrants, etc., and various items of public works equipment.

It is entirely feasible to purchase most supplies required in the operation of the several departments on contract instead of, as now, on open market order.

Storeroom Supplies Bought on Open Market Order

It is customary to buy a certain quantity of supplies for storeroom purposes. In 1912 supplies bought to stock the storeroom totaled $31,000. Records are maintained in the storeroom of receipts and deliveries, so that there is no reason why a contract should not be entered into for the supplies regularly kept at storerooms. This has not been done.

Buying in Small Lots

The advantages of central purchasing result not merely from the concentration of the function of purchasing in a single office, but from consolidating into single contracts all the supply and material requirements of the city of a particular trade classification. More advantageous terms result from joint purchases than can be obtained by individual departments buying small quantities independently. This advantage has not been availed of. Instead of anticipating their requirements the purchasing clerk is merely a shopper for the several departments, responding to their demands for supplies as requisitions are received from them.

City Buying Not Fully Centralized

The purchasing clerk buys for the police and fire departments, but he does not make purchases for the park department or the department of education, although these departments and the purchasing division are all located in the City Hall. The supplies required by the park department are practically of the same character as the supplies required for public works. There may be some reason, because of the special character of supplies required in the department of education, why that department should maintain its own purchasing agent, but there is no reason, beyond a tradition, why the park department should not utilize the purchasing agent once it is demonstrated that central purchasing actually effects economies.

No Analyses of Purchases Made

No analyses have been made of the kinds of supply of a similar nature purchased, nor has any attempt been made to forecast the requirements of the several departments in order that annual or quarterly contracts might be entered into.

It is suggested that steps be taken at once to analyze the purchases of the department for the year 1912, as a means of forecasting the requirements for the remainder of the present year and for the year 1914. The character of supplies required for the several departments does not vary greatly from year to year. An analysis of a year's consumption will furnish a fairly accurate basis for estimating the requirements of the year following.*

No Standards—No Specifications

No attempt has been made by the purchasing department to standardize the requirements of the different bureaus, nor, except in the case of coal, have specifications been provided to govern the quality of deliveries. In some cases samples are requested, and these are used to definitize purchase orders, but even in these cases no systematic attempt has been made by the purchasing clerk or comptroller to determine whether deliveries actually conform to samples.

Standarizing Means Economy

It is recommended that as soon as information is obtained of the supplies purchased for the consumption of the various depart-

---

* Such an analysis has been begun since this survey.

A clean alley is a convenience. An ill-kempt alley is a city nuisance.

A street cleaner in January.

ments during last year, standards be established for all supplies regularly required. Standardization means using the same grade of supply for the same purpose throughout all departments. Until soap, stationery, furniture, etc., are standardized the city will be penalized by permitting one department to requisition and obtain a more costly grade of a supply or material than another department has found it feasible to use for the same purpose.

Specifications

Specifications are essential not only to efficient buying but to efficient auditing. Following the selection of standards definite specifications should be prepared as a basis for future purchases.

Annual Contracts

For most supplies it is advantageous to make annual contracts at or about the beginning of the fiscal year. In the cases of certain supplies, such as coal and forage, where prices are governed by seasonal conditions, short term agreements should customarily be entered into in the season when the most favorable prices prevail. In certain other cases, such as perishable food stuffs, contracts should be made from month to month.

Partial Deliveries Under Annual Contracts

Objection is sometimes made to purchasing under annual supply contracts, on the theory that such contracts require delivery of total quantities of supplies purchased at a single time. This is not a valid objection for it is entirely feasible in such contracts to provide for partial deliveries of supplies as the need for their consumption arises.

Superintendent of Purchases Responsible to the Mayor

The position of purchasing agent is of sufficient importance to warrant the appointment of a superintendent of purchases, with special experience in purchasing work. The superintendent of purchases should not be subordinate to any administrative official for whose use he is required to buy supplies. He should be appointed by the mayor and should be responsible only to him.

City Engineer

Engineering Staff an Important Factor

In every branch of public works activities, questions of engineering play an important part. In an efficiently organized public works department, the engineering staff is the principal factor in planning, supervising and improving the methods of departmental work.

The present commissioner of public works is himself an engineer, but the multitude of administrative questions which he must consider necessarily prevents him from giving exclusive attention to the engineering problems of the department.

Position of City Engineer a Survival

The position of city engineer, now a survival and an anomaly, should be converted into the headship of the engineering staff of the department. Though " of " the department of public works, the city engineer is not " in " it. A ridiculous charter provision makes the position of city engineer practically worthless in so far as effective public works administration is concerned.

Charter Status of Office

Prior to the reorganization of the department of public works, the city engineer was president of the board of public works. Since then in all matters except those which relate to engineering questions coming up in the water department he has been made subordinate to the commissioner of public works. The charter specifically provides, however, that he shall not be a member of the department. A subordinate of the commissioner, the city engineer is appointed by the mayor. His term is three years, a year longer than the term of his immediate superior.

The grade and the curb. These are illustrations of highway problems.

Gutter bridges are dirt catchers.

The situation is aggravated by the fact that the office pays $4,000 a year, a salary equal to that of the mayor, and, next to the commissioner of public works, the highest in the city.

Legal Duties Unchanged

Though the act of 1907 removed the city engineer from the department of public works, it provided that he should continue to perform all duties devolved upon him by previous statutes. One of these duties was to " superintend and to do or cause to be done all the civil engineering required by the board of public works in the management and prosecution of all the public improvements committed to their charge ".

Actual Duties Limited

As a matter of fact, the present duties of the city engineer are practically confined to engineering work in the water department, because with regard to this work, the commissioner may not over-rule him. The operation of the water works is in the hands of an engineering superintendent, the activities of the city engineer being limited to construction work. In the language of one of the members of the department, in this work the city engineer is responsible to the " blue sky ".

Special Assistant in Charge of Engineering Work

The office of the city engineer contains a staff of draftsmen and estimators as well as three division engineers, who are all engaged on new construction work. Under the present administration this work has been removed from the supervision of the city engineer and placed in charge of a special assistant engineer, whose office was created by special ordinance, to be continued at the pleasure of the commissioner of public works. The division engineers should be made subordinate to the superintendent of street construction until such time as an engineering division is organized.*

---

*The commissioner of public works prefers the continuance of a separate organization for engineering work as a " check " on the bureau of street construction.

Chief Engineer instead of City Engineer

The office of city engineer should be abolished and the position of chief engineer created. The chief engineer would be subordinate to the commissioner of public works and in charge of all the engineering activities of the department. If the position of chief engineer is placed in the classified civil service list it will tend to become permanent, for commissioners of public works cannot expect in two years to obtain a complete grasp of the engineering problems of so large a city as Milwaukee. It now happens that the commissioner of public works is an engineer, but his term is only two years, and there is no assurance that his successor will be competent to direct the engineering activities of the department. It is highly important that there should be continuity of policy in engineering matters.

Bureau of Street Construction and Repair

Maintenance of Streets

Although there is great need for an extension of permanent pavements, many of the streets being poorly paved, the metropolitan size of the city, growing traffic and heightened demands of its residents will require increasingly careful attention to the problem of pavement maintenance. There are now laid in Milwaukee 104.28 miles of permanent pavements, exclusive of 271.04 miles of macadam. Of these, 30.72 miles are still under original contractors' guarantees, requiring that they be maintained without expense to the city, while 344.60 miles, on which the guarantee has expired, are maintained by city gangs.

Laws Handicap Pavement Maintenance

Under present laws pavement up-keep is seriously handicapped. An out-of-date statute unsuitable for a great city provides that the cost of paving and repaving shall be charged against abutting property until the sum of $3.00 per square yard has been assessed, and that thereafter half the cost shall be assessed. No assessments may be made unless the work is peti-

German cities make an effort to look well at depots. This is a winter greeting at one of Milwaukee's railway stations.

Year-round pavement repair would eliminate this condition.

tioned for by the property owners affected or consented to by a majority of the members of the council.

These provisions prevent the department from determining where repaving should be done in the light of traffic needs and the condition of the pavements.

Maintenance a City, Not a Local Problem

Local property owners or ward representatives should not be consulted in determining where and when a street should be repaved. This is primarily an engineering question, and should be governed by considerations of economy of maintenance and convenience of traffic. Moreover, it is unjust to property owners to charge them with the cost of repaving, because the deterioration of pavement is caused less by the use made of them by the owners of abutting property than by the general traffic of the city over which these owners have no control.

The pavements of a city exist primarily for the general convenience of the city. Once a permanent pavement is laid the cost of its repaving should be made a general charge.

Year Round Enforcement of Contract Guarantees

The 30.72 miles of pavement under guarantee are generally put in repair once a year. Early in the spring notices are sent to the responsible companies requiring them to make repairs on designated streets on or before May 15th. It is expected that by that day the companies will place the pavements for which they are responsible in perfect condition.

All contracts let require that repairs shall be made upon five days' notice *at any time*. There is, therefore, no reason why the guarantor companies should not be expected to keep the pavements, for which they are responsible, in repair throughout the year. It is suggested that these companies either arrange with the city to make the repairs or maintain plants in Milwaukee for the proper up-keep of their pavements throughout the year. It is feasible to make repairs in asphalt pavements practically at any season of the year, except when snow and rain prevent good workmanship.

Repairs of Streets on Which Guarantees Have Expired

Streets on which guarantees have expired consisting of 344.60 miles of pavement, are maintained by city gangs. In August, 1908, the city established an asphalt plant which provides material for the repair of asphalt streets by city gangs. The superintendent of repairs, by general inspection, determines the locations at which repairs are to be made. No definite plan of work is laid out but the gangs are sent from street to street, as the superintendent determines.

An Inspection System Suggested

A system of inspection should be established by the city for the prompt reporting of all pavement defects.

For the purpose of pavement inspection, it is suggested that the city be divided into districts, and that an inspector be assigned to each district. These inspectors should report daily on prescribed forms the exact location of all defects in pavements of their districts. Inspectors' reports should be reviewed in the office of the superintendent of repairs. From these reports a schedule of work should be prepared both for the guarantor contractors and for the city repair gangs. After repairs, reinspections should be made to determine satisfactoriness of work. If repairs were systematically made in this way for at least nine months of the year, the streets of the city might be kept in practically perfect condition. Economy would result from this " stitch in time " method because the large holes which disfigure the streets, impede traffic, and raise the cost of repairs, result from neglect to repair small holes when they first appear.

The Police as Highway Inspectors

It may be found feasible to utilize the police more effectively than they are at present used to report pavement defects.

Milwaukee has numerous grade crossings. These should be eliminated before congestion of population and traffic makes them not only an inconvenience, but a menace to life.

Rule 57 of the police regulations provides:

> " The lieutenant shall have general charge of his precinct, visiting every part of it as often as once each week, noting the condition of the streets, sidewalks, street-lights, obstructions, nuisances, and non-compliance with the city ordinances, and all other matters requiring the attention of the police in his precinct and all matters which require the attention of the board of public works and the board of health."

Lieutenants may not have time on their weekly tour to report all pavement defects in sufficient detail to furnish the basis for proper repair work. Patrolmen, however, should report accurately all principal defects and these should be checked by lieutenants.

Centralize Street Construction

New street construction is carried on in part by the division engineers, formerly under the supervision of the city engineer, and in part by the bureau of construction and repairs.

With the growing importance of repair work, it is suggested that a special division or bureau of paving maintenance be established, and that all work relating to the construction of pavements be placed under the supervision of the superintendent of street construction.

A Work Program

Under the charter, the commissioner of public works is required to formulate annually for the consideration of the common council, a plan of improvements for the several wards. This plan, after approval by the council, governs the new construction work of the department for the year in question.

It is suggested that the department of public works make a comprehensive study of the prospective paving needs of Milwaukee for a period of five years, and that a program of improvements be determined upon, according to which the new construction work of the department may be conducted. By this means land owners will be advised of prospective charges against their land, and a properly considered and harmonious plan of improvement substituted for the piecemeal plans adopted by successive administrations.

As a basis for the proposed plan of improvements, it is suggested that a careful study be made of the street plan of the city. This study should include consideration of the prospective needs for additional thoroughfares in the downtown section, and of contemplated development of outlying sections.

A Pavement Policy

A definite policy should govern the determination of the kind of pavement to be laid on a particular street. Factors to be considered in reaching a determination are:

1. Conditions to which the pavement will be subjected

    a Climate
    b Volume of traffic
    c Kind of traffic
    d Grade of street
    e Character of district
    f Presence of car tracks

2. Qualities of pavement

    a Durability
    b Smoothness
    c Noiselessness
    d Slipperiness
    e Cleanliness
    f Cost

Sub-Surface Maps

The present practice of the bureau of street construction of requiring property owners to make gas, sewer and water connections prior to the permanent improvement of streets, is an excellent step in the direction of preventing unnecessary disturbance of street surfaces. Further to minimize preventable destruction of pavements by public service corporations, the water department, or plumbers, it is suggested that sub-surface maps be prepared showing the precise location and character of structures under the surface of the city streets. The possession of maps of

A city street unfit for traffic, but water continuously running for the weary traveler.   This water waste costs many dollars from April to November.

this character will enable the department to control intelligently the issuance of permits for street excavations. Sub-surface maps will become increasingly useful as the number of pipes and conduits under the street increases.

Repair of Park Roads

Roads under the jurisdiction of the park board should be placed in the care of the bureau of street construction and repair, in order that the same standards that now apply to highways without the parks may be applied to those within them. A step in the direction of centralization was taken this year when unpaved city roads, formerly under the care of the several ward superintendents, were placed under the bureau of street construction.

Contractors Gamble on Payment

Contractors constructing street improvements are not paid directly out of the city treasury, except for work which is chargeable to the city as a whole. Certificates are issued for that part of the work which is assessable against property benefited. These certificates contractors deposit with the city treasurer, who collects the amounts due upon them from the individual property owners.

In certain cities street improvement contractors are paid directly out of a fund created by the issuance of assessment bonds. By using the city's instead of the contractor's credit to finance improvements more favorable contract terms are likely to be obtained and property owners bearing the assessment would receive the benefit of the city's ability to borrow at lower rates of interest than can the average contractor. The certificate method of payment further increases the cost of improvements, because the contractor is obliged to assume the risk of deferred payments. Since certificates do not become due until an improvement is completed, the contractor receives no progress payments and must therefore add to his bid price the cost of financing the complete undertaking. This condition will be partly corrected by legislation obtained by the city at the 1913 session of the legislature which permits property owners to pay their assessments as the work is completed.

Street Signs Inadequate

Milwaukee's streets are poorly signed, both in respect of the number and character of signs used. Even in the downtown section, small signs, which are inconspicuous and cheap-looking, are used. Good street signs are indispensable aids to strangers and often a great convenience to residents.

Sidewalk and Street Encumbrance

From inspection, sidewalks and streets are frequently encumbered with private property. This should not occur except by special permit, as in the case of building construction. If necessary, the department of public works should provide special inspectors to keep sidewalks free for passage of pedestrians, and streets clear of obstructions to traffic.

Bureau of Sanitation

Ward Division a Survival

All work of this bureau, except the collection and incineration of garbage, is under the supervision of twenty-six ward superintendents. Each of the ward superintendents is in a measure a local superintendent of street cleaning and sprinkling, sewer basin cleaning and ash collection. Each ward superintendent selects his own laborers from a civil service list, without supervision of the superintendent of the bureau. Each ward superintendent hires, on his own judgment, horses and carts to remove ashes and street sweepings, and employs drivers and teams to remove the material taken from sewer basins, to drive sweeper and flushing machines, etc. Each ward superintendent determines in a large degree for himself the manner in which his work is to be performed, although he is subject to the continuous supervision of the superintendent of the bureau.

An inexpensive but legible and attractive street sign, now used in New York City.

The ward organization of the bureau of street cleaning is a survival of the time when the ward, instead of the entire city, was regarded as a unit of activity. Being the units of local representation in the common council, ward lines are primarily established for political purposes. Those who frame them naturally do not consider them in the light of a sub-division of the city for the efficient execution of public works.

Districts for Street Cleaning Needed

It is suggested that steps be taken at once scientifically to re-district the city for the work of street cleaning so as to reduce the number of local superintendents, and at the same time to assign to each superintendent an approximately equal amount of work. The mere fact that the work of the department is sub-divided by wards furnishes a continuing inducement to political interference with its activities. This is evidenced by the fact that ward superintendents are permitted to distribute to the residents of their wards the patronage of making minor repairs to equipment. Ward superintendents are expected, so far as possible, to hire their horses and carts from the residents of their wards.

The problem of street cleaning should be considered from the standpoint of the city as a whole, and not from the standpoint of political wards.

Twenty-six Standards of Labor Efficiency

Under present methods laborers are selected from lists prepared by the civil service commission. No tests, however, are applied to applicants except that they must not be more than 62 years of age. The civil service commission places the names of applicants upon the eligible lists in the order they are received. Thereafter, appointments are supposed to be made in the order of application. Ward superintendents, however, are free to dismiss men who do not meet their individual requirements. The result is that there exist either no standards of labor efficiency or twenty-six different standards, according to the individual judgment of the ward superintendents. Under present conditions the most efficient ward superintendents refuse to employ old men who are unable to do a full day's work, or to protect themselves against the dangers of traffic in streets. Other ward superintendents with less initiative accept laborers assigned to them and consequently perform their work at a greater cost to the city. The superintendent of street cleaning should personally, or through representatives subject to his direction at the central office, employ all laborers and assign them to the different ward superintendents.

Rules for the guidance of all employees should be framed and a system of fines and penalties prescribed.

Service records should be kept for each employee in which notation should be made of discipline imposed and periodic ratings of work efficiency.

Payrolls as Pensions

There is still a tendency in Milwaukee to adhere to the ancient practice of treating a city payroll as a refuge for the indigent and infirm. To place on the city payrolls old men who find it difficult to obtain other employment is not only an unscientific method of public relief, but works injury to the entire city through lowering the efficiency of the city service. The superintendent of street cleaning would probably be able to save a sufficient sum by the use of strong, efficient workmen, to pension every old man now on the city payroll actually in need of this form of relief.

Pay Day Time Loss

Street laborers, sweepers, etc., are required to report for monthly payment at the various ward yards, there to meet the paymaster. This method causes considerable loss of time. Where men work in gangs the location of the gangs can easily be made known to the paymaster so that payments can be made to the men at their places of work. Where payment in the field is not possible, the paymaster should arrange to meet the men either at the beginning or towards the close of the day so that a minimum of time may be lost.

Many of Milwaukee's curb gutters are in bad condition. Good street cleaning keeps gutters scrupulously clean.

Delayed Wages

Payrolls are not prepared and paid with suitable promptness. Ward laborers paid monthly, we were informed, frequently receive their checks two or three weeks after the end of the period to which they apply. These delays for men receiving $2.00 a day and having families dependent upon them, impose genuine hardship. This condition is largely due, we were informed, to delays incident to the approval of payrolls by aldermen. If the budget were properly prepared there would be no need for aldermanic approval of payrolls.

Equipment Standards

The bureau of sanitation has minimized the danger of laxity of standards in respect of its hired equipment by providing boxes for wagons used for sewer basins and cleanings, and ash collection and the removal of street sweepings. No standards, however, are exacted for horses supplied, either with respect to age, weight or soundness. These should be established in order that maximum service may be obtained.

Centralize Equipment Repair

The superintendent, in addition to providing minimum specifications for hired horses, and exercising care in the selection of the laboring force, should take under his central control the maintenance and repair of all city-owned equipment. It would probably be found profitable to establish a central repair shop, or to have all city equipment repaired at one of the city shops already established—for example in the fire department.

Ward superintendents should have no discretion in respect of these matters, and should not be placed in a position where they may subordinate the interests of the city to local favoritism, however well-intentioned.

Uniforms for Cleaners

Street cleaners are not now required to wear uniforms.* Uniforms were experimented with some time ago, but abandoned be-

---

* This practice has been resumed in downtown sections of the city since our survey.

cause of the expense their up-keep imposed upon the men. This expense is not considerable and if necessary, should be borne by the city, in order that the advantages in service resulting from the use of uniforms may be obtained. These advantages not only consist in developing public interest in the street cleaner's work and making him conspicuous, thus protecting him in streets where traffic is congested, but in developing in the force itself a corps spirit. The use of white uniforms is now practically universal in large cities, and is a mark of progressiveness which Milwaukee should promptly adopt.

Efficiency from Comparison of Records of Cost and Equipment

On monthly time reports ward superintendents are required to present an inventory of equipment on hand at the beginning of the month, disposed of during the month, and on hand at the end of the month. These reports are filed, but are not analyzed in order to establish comparisons of the use of equipment between the several ward superintendents.

It is suggested that for each quarter a schedule be prepared, showing the cost and quantity of material and amount of equipment used in the several wards. Other statements showing, for example, the cost per square yard of streets cleaned, sprinkled and oiled, according to kind of pavement, the cost per yard of sewer basins cleaned and the cost per cubic yard of ashes and street sweepings removed, should be circularized for the information and stimulation of superintendents. In this way wholesome competition will be established and the superintendents given helpful information on the cost of their work.

Conferences on Work Methods

It is suggested that from time to time conferences between the bureau superintendent and all ward superintendents be held, in order that uniformity of work methods may be obtained, and discussion of opportunities for improvement may be encouraged.

An uncovered ash cart. An unnecessary annoyance to citizens.

Covers for Ash Wagons

Except in one or two experimental cases, wagons used for the removal of ashes and street sweepings are not now covered. The superintendent has under consideration the provision of covers for these wagons. This should be done promptly, since the blowing about of ashes and street sweepings is a source of discomfort to citizens, and is easily and cheaply prevented by the use of tarpaulin covers. For use in ash collection it may be feasible to adopt a type of wagon commonly used in German cities. This wagon is so constructed as completely to prevent ashes from blowing when cans are emptied. Householders are required to provide receptacles which fit with precision into apertures in the cover of the wagon.

Year Round Cleaning

Street cleaning, except in the downtown district, is practically abandoned during the winter months. All paved streets should be cleaned throughout the year.

More Cans for Sweeping

In the spring of the year a general clean-up of the streets is undertaken. The survey was made at the time of resumption of active street cleaning work. It was observed in many localities that cans were not provided for street sweepings, and that piles of dirt and manure were permitted to lie for some time along the margins of the streets. An adequate number of receptacles for sweepings should be placed on the streets at the beginning of the season.

A Trial of Automobile Trucks Suggested

It is suggested that an experiment be tried in the use of ten ton automobile trucks for the removal of ashes and street sweepings, where the roads leading to the dumps are suitable for motor vehicles of this size.

More Frequent Garbage Collections

In summer garbage collections are made from households once a week, and from November to April once every ten days. Particularly during the summer months, it seems desirable in a city of the size of Milwaukee that household garbage should be collected at least twice a week, as is now done for boarding houses and hotels in the downtown districts.

Ward Lines Ignored in Garbage Collection

In garbage collection, in contradistinction to the work of street cleaning, the city is treated as a unit and the entire work of collection is under the supervision of a central superintendent. Ward lines have been completely ignored.

Control of Receptacles in Wrong Department

Householders are required to use metal garbage receptacles, but the health department, now responsible for seeing that these are provided, does not strictly enforce the requirement. It is suggested that the enforcement of this rule be transferred from the health department to the bureau of sanitation.

Incineration Plant

The superintendent of sanitation informs us that an effort is being made to reduce the cost of incineration to a minimum. Because of limited time we were unable to investigate the question of costs and efficiency of the incineration plant. We have undertaken to make a comparison of incineration costs at various plants throughout the country and purpose submitting a supplementary memorandum on this subject.

Rules and Regulations Needed

In order to standardize and increase the efficiency of street cleaning and garbage and ash collection throughout the city, it is suggested that the superintendent prepare and issue a definite set of departmental regulations. These regulations would pre-

More cans are needed for street sweepings.

scribe in detail the duties and responsibilities of superintendents, drivers, sweepers, dump foremen, etc., and lay a basis for discipline and efficient supervision. Without rules the superintendent is at the mercy of foremen and the ward foremen at the mercy of their subordinates.

Bureau of Bridges and Public Buildings

City Force for Repair of Buildings

A bridge squad makes repairs to bridges and certain repairs to public buildings. A general repair squad should be organized, equipped to make all current repairs to bridges and to all city buildings.

For the purpose of making repairs public buildings are said to be inspected annually. As yet no record of these inspections has been kept. A form for inspections should be prepared and all buildings subjected to a thorough examination at least once a year.

No Repair Cost Records

Suitable cost records are not kept of repairs made by laborers in the employ of the bureau. The superintendent intends to give early attention to the provision of cost records. Until this is done the relative economy of making repairs by contract and by departmental labor cannot be ascertained.

Centralize Public Building Construction

School and park buildings are not constructed under the supervision of this bureau, though fire stations and police stations are. Despite the separate organization of school and park boards, it would probably prove economical to centralize in a single department all building construction paid for by taxpayers.

Private Building Cleaning Costs vs. City Cost

No comparative studies have been made of the cost of cleaning City Hall and other city buildings with the cost of cleaning similar buildings under private control. Comparisons of this nature usually result in lowering the cost of cleaning public buildings.

Rules for Cleaning Needed

No detailed regulations have been laid down to govern the work of building cleaning.

Model Steam Plant for City Hall

Attention has not been given to the efficiency of the steam and lighting plant in the City Hall building. Up to date even the amount of current annually generated by the plant has not been metered. All coal used should be carefully weighed, and water, steam and electricity metered. The City Hall heating and lighting plant should be a model in efficient and economical operation.

Street Lighting

Control of the street lighting system has been assigned to this bureau, but so far no steps have been taken to establish a proper system of light inspection or to study the question of street lighting.

At the time of the survey the whole question of street lighting was in an unsettled condition, due to a recent legal controversy over the establishment of a municipal lighting plant. Efficient street lighting is a matter of scientific selection and location of lamps plus careful inspection.

Whether street lighting is supplied by contract or by the city lighting plant, supervision of the location of lights and the efficiency of service should be an important future function of this bureau.

Control over Equipment

An annual inventory is taken of equipment but no use is made of it. Although the City Hall janitors and other caretakers of buildings are responsible for all property in their care, neither the bureau nor the caretakers are currently informed of what this property consists.

Sometimes machinery is not labor saving. Because of faulty construction, the operation of this sweeper requires two men. The driver should both drive and control the broom.

Office Directory for City Hall

The City Hall is not provided with office directories. A directory of offices located on the floor in question should be conspicuously displayed on each floor. At the four street entrances, of the City Hall general directories of all floors should be provided.

POLICE DEPARTMENT

A Permanent Police Chief

New York City has had eight heads of the police force in eleven years. Since 1888 Milwaukee's police department has had one head, the present chief. Permanency in the headship of police departments is a requisite to efficient control of the force. In Europe, police heads retain their positions practically for life. The efficiency of Milwaukee's police department is doubtless attributable to the fact that the police chief has been kept long enough fully to master his duties and to carry out a consistent policy of administration.

Suggestions Based on Approved Practices

The science of policing a large city is rapidly undergoing development. Police administration in large cities throughout the world is receiving the attention of specialists. Irrespective of the personal efficiency of police officials, progressive police departments should avail themselves of the experience of other cities in adopting new methods as they are proved more efficient than the old. The New York Bureau of Municipal Research has recently made a study of police administration in New York City and in ten principal European cities. Suggestions made regarding the police department of Milwaukee, although not intended at this time to be in any sense complete, are based upon approved practices of other large communities.

School for Recruits

In 1910, 64 new appointments to the force were made and 40 in 1911. The 1910 appointments were made on four different dates in groups of from 14 to 18 at a single time. The 1911 appointments were made on three different dates in groups of 13, 13 and 14 respectively. For these two years, therefore, excepting for a single odd appointment on May 2, 1910, admissions to the force were made in groups ranging from 13 to 18 men. The practice of appointing a group of men to the force simultaneously makes it feasible to conduct a systematic recruit school. A police lieutenant now gives instruction in the police manual, military drill, and pistol practice. While useful, such instruction does not fulfill the requirements of modern police training.

Establish a Training School for Patrolmen

Before recruits are admitted to active police duty it is suggested that they be placed in a recruit school for full time for a period of from 30 to 90 days. A carefully planned scheme of instruction should be established and competent instructors employed. In the school recruits should be taught laws and ordinances, court room practice, methods of handling prisoners, jiujitsu, military drill, swimming, pistol practice, report writing, identification of persons, first aid, finger printing, and they should be given practical instruction in patrolling, regulation of traffic, noting violation of ordinances, etc.

In New York City all recruits are required to attend a school of instruction for 30 days after appointment. In London a six weeks' training course is given; in Düsseldorf, Germany, a 12 weeks' course; and in Vienna, a 12 months' course.

Careful training of the recruits of the police force is the best means of securing a high grade police service. Modern policing requires not only physical strength, endurance and courage, but sympathetic understanding of conditions which create crime, and ability to deal constructively with them.

In addition to instruction for new members, the school should conduct courses for all members of the force keeping them informed of new ordinances, statutes, etc., and in touch with advanced police methods.

Medical Examination

Patrolmen before admission to the force are required to undergo at their own expense a physical examination by a physician designated by the department. This examination should be paid for by the city. No candidate should be permitted to give any consideration whatsoever to the physician who determines his fitness for police duty.

Medical examinations are deferred until applicants have passed all other examinations and present themselves for appointment. Examinations should be given when men first apply, as well as immediately before appointment, so that remediable conditions may be corrected and time saved the applicant if defects appearing are not remediable.

In 1911, out of 56 applicants who passed the preliminary examination, ten, or 17.85%, failed to pass the medical examination.

A Ten Hour Shift

The patrol is now divided into three shifts from 6 P. M. to 2 A. M., 12 M. to 8 A. M., and 7 A. M. to 6 P. M. The long day shift is interrupted by one hour off for dinner. The day shift, therefore, consists of two five hour tours of duty. Efficient patrolling requires alertness and enthusiasm. Even at the cost of increasing the force it is questionable whether tours longer than eight hours are profitable.

Patrolmen's Notebooks

Patrolmen are required by rule to keep memorandum books for their personal use to record observations and acts. No standard notebooks, however, are provided by the department. Good practice requires that patrolmen keep full notes of violations of law observed by them and all facts relating to arrests, accidents and other important occurrences. These notebooks should be in loose leaf form, each sheet being numbered at the end of each tour of duty. The sheets properly signed and containing all notes made on the tour should be turned in to the station officer and by him reviewed and filed as official records.

Patrolmen and Sergeants Should Check Each Other

Sergeants and patrolmen should both be required to enter in their notebooks the place and time of their meeting and each should sign or initial the other's entry. The record may then be reviewed and used as a check on the sergeant as well as the patrolman.

All Violations Noted Not Reported

Patrolmen are not required to report all violations noted but are permitted to use their discretion as to whether a matter should be called to the attention of their superiors. If the patrolman is able to persuade the offender to correct the violation he is not required to report it to his superior officer. All violations noted should be reported and the fact of correction stated if the patrolman is able to have them corrected. Otherwise the patrolman is given undue power of discrimination in law enforcement.

If any class of violation is regarded as too trivial for report, as, for example, violations of rules of the road, these should be specifically exempted.

Reports Often Informal

In many cases patrolmen's reports are now made on odd sheets of paper. Forms should be provided for all conditions concerning which patrolmen are customarily required to submit reports. These forms should be placed in a binder of a size convenient for pocket use, and should prescribe the minimum information required for an intelligent understanding of the matter reported upon.

Sergeants' Reports Informal

Sergeants are permitted to report informally both infractions of rules by patrolmen and violations of laws by citizens. If any matter is worthy of report it is worthy of a written report. All reports of sergeants should be in writing. This is especially important in regard to reports bearing on patrolmen's conduct, since such reports furnish the best basis for departmental discipline and for keeping patrolmen's efficiency records.

Complaints Against Force

According to rule, complaints against members of the force are required to bear the signature of the complainant "before the same shall be investigated". According to a statement by the chief, this rule is not strictly enforced, all complaints received being investigated. It seems desirable, however, that the rule should be modified so as to omit the provision quoted. Anonymous complaints are often the most valuable sources of information. As a means of informing the chief and other commanding officers of the dereliction of patrolmen, citizens' complaints are of great value.

Complaints against members of the force are investigated by the inspector in charge of the force. It is suggested that they may be investigated by a confidential subordinate of the chief. The chief should be provided with a high grade aide who could help not only in improving the morale of the force, but in studying and instituting means of increasing the general efficiency of the department.

Action on Complaints

In 1911, 34 complaints against officers were heard by the chief of police. Only two of the accused were found not guilty; 11 were dismissed, two for drinking and intoxication; four were fined for drinking and frequenting saloons; one was fined five days' pay for intoxication. No officer found guilty of intoxication should be continued on the force.

"Look Out" Notices Should Be Printed

Announcements of persons wanted or "look out" notices are read to the members of the force over the telephone. It is exteremely difficult for most men to remember detailed descriptions of persons wanted. It is suggested that the department print descriptions of persons wanted, furnishing them to all members of the force, and require that these descriptions be placed in a loose leaf notebook to be carried by patrolmen. In case of important criminals wanted reprints of photographs should be furnished as well. When persons called for on previous announcements are arrested, notice should be given to all officers in order that they may remove the names of arrested persons from their lists. In Philadelphia, the practice has recently been adopted of including in this general notice to members of the force, a commendation of the particular officer who made the arrest. The practice has resulted in improvement of the corps spirit of the department.

Mounted Patrolmen

Milwaukee has no mounted patrolmen although they are desired by the chief who states that he has repeatedly asked for an allowance to employ them. Mounted patrolmen are useful in controlling crowds on occasions of special congestion, such as parades, and in patrolling outlying districts. In less thickly settled sections of the city, a mounted officer is able to cover territory more frequently than a foot patrolman, and thus increases the sense of assurance of persons living in isolated homes. Moreover, mounted patrolmen stationed on the boulevards and drives are useful in checking runaways. Cycle patrolmen are not an adequate substitute for mounted police, for cyclists cannot be used advantageously throughout the year.

Trained Police Dogs Should Be Tried

It is suggested that the police department employ trained police dogs as aids to patrolmen in outlying districts. A single patrolman with a trained police dog is rated by many police experts as more effective than two officers patrolling together. Trained dogs are used extensively in European police departments and have been found most efficient.

Identification System

Bertillon measurements, photographs and finger prints are kept of persons arrested on serious charges. Measurements are carefully made. The department gallery will become increasingly useful as an aid to identification of criminals. The department utilizes the collection of criminal measurements maintained by the national bureau of identification at Washington.

Identification from Facial Characteristics

Rule 87 of the department requires a patrolman to watch the conduct of all persons known to be of bad character and " fix in his mind such impressions as will enable him to recognize them when he meets them in the streets at night ". This is a difficult feat even for an exceptionally capable officer. All patrolmen, and particularly those assigned to detective work, should be taught methods of identification from facial characteristics. A very definite science of identification by type of nose, ear lobe, forehead, etc., has been worked out and is readily learned by an intelligent patrolman. To make rule 87 effective, a description of the facial characteristics of all persons of suspicious character whom it is desired the police shall keep under scrutiny, should be placed in the hands of patrolmen in printed form, in order that they may not only observe, but actually identify such suspicious persons.

System of Fining a Hardship for Families

Delinquent patrolmen are punished by fines deducted from their pay. Patrolmen were fined in all over 80 days' pay during 1911. This method of punishment is common in police departments but tends to shift the burden of punishment from the offenders to their families. It is recommended that consideration be given to the question of whether punishment by assignment to special and particularly unpleasant and laborious duty would not be a more efficacious method. Revocation of days off is also an alternative method of disciplining delinquent officers.

Wrong Pension Fund Practice

A pension fund established under statute provides for the retirement on half-pay of members of the force serving 22 years.

The fund is made up of deductions of 2½% of the monthly salaries of members of the police department, and 1% of all revenues collected by the city from all licenses, except dog licenses. To a considerable extent, therefore, the revenues of the fund are uncertain since the number of licenses that will be taken out cannot be foretold. It is bad finance to divert, without appropriation, any portion of the city's revenues to special purposes. All revenues should be paid into the general fund and appropriated by the council out of that fund. The present income of the pension fund is insufficient to establish a proper reserve and to care for existing pensions now chargeable against it. This is a matter that demands immediate attention. A study should be made of the average length of service of former members of the force, and present and prospective liability, in order that an *actuarial* basis may be established for developing the fund. Supplementing the 2½% deductions from the salaries·of the force the city should appropriate a sum exactly sufficient to provide for all prospective liabilities.

Efficiency Records Lacking

Individual service records are not now kept either for detectives or for patrolmen. Records should be established showing for patrolmen, among other things, the following:

> Name
> Badge number
> Previous occupation
> Age on admission to the force
> Weight on admission to the force
> Height
> Civil service rating
> Rating in school of instruction
> Assignments by precincts
> Promotions
> Demotions
> Special services rendered
> Commendations
> Reprimands
> Fines
> Suspension
> Sick leave

For each detective, in addition to the foregoing facts, careful record should be kept of cases investigated, arrests made as a result of such investigation, property recovered and convictions obtained.

Bad Sanitary Conditions

The sanitary condition of the central station house is deplorable, particularly the cells. The people have authorized a bond issue for a new building but no appropriation has been made. This is a matter that the city should not longer neglect.

The sanitary condition of the cell house of station No. 3 is even more deplorable than that of the central station. This cell house is unfit for use and should be closed at once.

Insufficient Station Houses

Milwaukee has at present only five station houses. Detroit with a population of 465,766 has eleven station houses. The chief of police states that five additional houses are urgently needed. It now requires half an hour by car, or twice that long by foot, for patrolmen to go from the station house to certain posts. This obviously is a serious waste of time.

More Matrons Needed

There is but one police matron for the entire city and she is attached to the central station. Although women prisoners requiring the services of a matron are usually taken to the central station, many women prisoners are detained at the other four station houses where there are no matrons.

No woman prisoner should be detained in a station house unless there is a matron attached to it. Either additional matrons should be appointed or all women prisoners should be sent to the central station. In many states the detention of women prisoners in a station house where there is no matron is prohibited by law.

A Juvenile Problem Apparent

The fact that more than 11% of all persons arrested in 1911 (the last year for which a report is available) were under 21 years of age shows clearly that Milwaukee, in common with other great cities, needs to give attention to the city's youth, especially with reference to recreation, home conditions, and training in good citizenship.

Police Report

The 1911 report is the last published official statement of the police department's work. The report consists chiefly of statistical tables, many of which contain valuable information. This information is not always so presented, however, as to convey its full significance to the public. Because of the peculiar importance of police reports the following suggestions with reference to the report, are made:

1. The report contains no textual matter, nor any statement of the chief or the board of police commissioners on police conditions of the city or on special problems of the department. No review is given of improvements made in the administration of the department during the year, nor are suggestions made for promoting its efficiency. The chief states that, finding recommendations futile, some years ago, he ceased to make them. The annual report furnishes a special opportunity to the police chief and to the police board for calling public attention to police needs. With public interest in the work of the police department, such as the proposed Citizens' Bureau should be able to stimulate, it should prove helpful in obtaining support for the department if the report discussed program, new undertakings and pressing needs

2. No information is given in the report of the expenditures of the department, nor of the value of buildings or equipment under its control. Fifteen pages now given to printing the names of members of the department could be used very advantageously for presenting important financial and statistical information now lacking. Without knowledge of costs comparative efficiency cannot be tested. Not only what is done but what it costs to do it should be told

3. A detailed table covering 13 pages is given of arrests made by the police department. No information is given, however, of the number of complaints received by the department upon which arrests were based, so that it is impossible to determine the extent of the department's efficiency. Thus, 11 arrests were made for murder, but no information is given of the number of murder cases reported to the police department. It is therefore impossible to say whether the efficiency of the department in detecting murders was 50% or 75% or 100%. Complaints received of crimes committed should be compared with arrests made as a result of such complaints. It is suggested that arrests made on the initiative of the department, without the receipt of complaints, be shown separately

4. Tables giving the disposition of cases show only whether the prisoners were discharged or found guilty, and if guilty, the nature of the sentence. They do not show, however, how many murderers were convicted and how many discharged, how many burglars were convicted and how many discharged. For no crime is the number of convictions and discharges compared with the number of persons charged with that crime. Such information would definitize public understanding of results obtained by the department

5. The table of the disposition of cases shows those discharged and those found guilty, and for those found guilty whether sentenced or fined. No information is given as to amount of fine or length of sentence.

6. No table is given to show whether persons arrested had been previously arrested, and if so, the nature of the previous charge and its disposition. This information helps locate the source of crime and is of value both to the police and the public

7. Six pages are devoted to a chronological list of fugitives from justice arrested in Milwaukee and turned over to authorities in other cities. No reason appears for printing the names of persons arrested. A brief summary of arrest by classes of crime would indicate the activity of the department in this respect

8. A page is devoted to a table of nativity of persons arrested. It seems desirable that this information be classified by general character of the crime, as, for example, violation of corporation ordinance, statutory misdemeanor or felony, for which the arrest was made

9. Tables are provided of age, social condition and race of persons arrested. It is likewise suggested that these be classified by character of arrest and disposition

10. Though patrolmen are required to report all street lamps not burning to the department of public works, no information is given in the annual report of the number of such reports. The importance of this work to public safety and convenience would seem to warrant its inclusion in the police report

11. It would be useful to include in the annual report a comparative table of complaints, arrests, convictions, etc., compared with similar data for other large American cities

12. The report contains no information of work done by the detectives as distinguished from the remainder of the force. At present it is impossible to learn the number of arrests due to detectives' work, or the number of convictions obtained as a result of the activity of detectives

13. No information is obtained in the report on administration or condition of the police pension fund. It is desirable that this be shown in detail, including existing pensions, pensions discontinued, granted, and reasons for action taken

FIRE DEPARTMENT

Periodic Efficiency Tests

Unlike other departments of the city government, fire departments in large cities are periodically examined by experts under orders to find and report all conditions showing lack of efficiency. These examinations are made by the National Board of Fire Underwriters, representing the fire insurance companies. Because these companies depend upon fire departments to protect them from excessive loss, they have a peculiar and continuing interest in maintaining the fire-fighting efficiency of fire departments. The underwriters naturally give more attention to equipment, organization and fire-fighting methods than they do to the administrative and economy aspects of the department, but these they by no means neglect.

Conditions Promoting Efficiency

These underwriters' examinations put into the hands of department chiefs concrete suggestions for increasing departmental efficiency. Moreover, fire department work from its nature is continually subject to public operation and test. These conditions, as well as an efficient personnel, have contributed to the establishment of a well organized and well conducted fire department in Milwaukee.

Underwriters Call Department Efficient

It so happened that a short time before the survey of the Bureau of Municipal Research, the National Board of Fire Underwriters made an exhaustive study of the Milwaukee fire department. This examination covered the months of September, October and November, 1912, and was made by four engineers. The conclusion of these experts, stated briefly, was that the fire department " is an efficient force, well equipped and maintained and fairly well supported financially. The department is under satisfactory supervision and is managed by capable officers, who are firemen of long experience and excellent reputation. The methods employed in appointment and promotions, in conjunction with the drills and probationary system, have resulted in an efficient and well officered force."

Bureau's Impression Favorable

In detail, general commendation is given to the operation of the various branches of the department. The conclusion reached by the National Board of Fire Underwriters agrees with impressions gained by us in a brief examination of the fire department. This examination, limited to several hours' questioning of the chief, of which a stenographic record was made, showed, according to statements made by the chief, that methods employed in Milwaukee are for the most part in conformance with good practice elsewhere.

A Long Tenure Chief

The present head of the department has been a member of the force for 27 years and with the exception of one year has occupied the position of chief since 1905. As in the case of the police department the chief has been given time to formulate and carry out a policy of administration. The demonstration made in the police and fire departments of the beneficial effect of long tenures should lead to the establishment of indefinite tenures for all important administrative positions.

Business Methods Need Further Study

Because the Board of Fire Underwriters does not give extensive attention to the business aspects of fire administration these should receive further study than we were able to give them. We have, however, no information to show that the business methods of the department are inefficient.

A Commendable Practice

The department deserves commendation for using the uniformed force to make repairs to station houses and equipment. In 1911 the equivalent of 1,419 days of eight hours each or the total working time of more than five men was devoted to repair work.

No Departmental Physician

The department has no staff physician to care for injured firemen, to attend them in sickness and to supervise their health. A departmental physician is desirable not only to aid in controlling absences because of illness, but to supervise the general health of the firemen, the sanitary condition of station houses, etc.

Fire Prevention Needs Strengthening

The most important feature of modern fire fighting is fire prevention. Fire prevention work in Milwaukee is divided between three agencies—the state fire marshal, the city building bureau and the fire department. These three bodies have not agreed upon a plan of coöperation as they should do. The fire department has no power to compel structural changes in buildings. It can, however, advise and if necessary persuade owners to remove rubbish and to correct other conditions which promote the hazard of fire.

District chiefs, of whom there are six, are required to inspect or to cause to be inspected all buildings in their respective districts, except dwelling houses, both to acquire a knowledge of the character of buildings and to recommend to owners and occupants of buildings action that would tend to reduce the liability of fire. Besides the district chiefs, two disabled firemen are sent through the city to inspect buildings for fire risks.

During the months of May and June, when the streets of the city were torn up for public works improvements, the department, as a measure of precaution, caused the inspection of all buildings in the fourth ward. The fire chief reports that, during the period of inspection, the total number of fires occurring was reduced 25% for May and 50% for June when compared with the number occurring in the same months last year. It seems fair to credit to inspection at least a portion of this reduction.

The result of the experiment conducted in May and June amply demonstrates the desirability of continuing rigorous systematic fire prevention inspection throughout the year.

District chiefs are not required to make a report to the chief engineer, of conditions found, unless their " recommendations are disregarded ".

In reply to a question regarding the effectiveness of existing fire prevention ordinances, the chief said: " I must confess that Milwaukee is backward in that respect. We have various ordinances and state laws, but usually, when we come to test them, they are found defective."

The fire department should make inspections not less than once a year of all buildings for manufacturing and mercantile purposes, all loft buildings, theatres or buildings used for the purpose of assemblage, all tenements and dwelling houses in congested districts, and should be given power to enforce its orders.

House to House Inspections

Members of the uniformed force may be used to make house to house inspection, as in Philadelphia and Cincinnati. In Philadelphia uniformed firemen made 25,000 inspections from Febru-

95

ary 15 to June 1, 1913. Conditions which they desired remedied were pointed out to the occupants of buildings while the firemen were still in the building. In no case did the occupant resent or refuse to comply with the suggestion given. From this it appears that if the work is handled properly people are only too willing to eliminate fire hazards in their own quarters.

The work done in Philadelphia might very properly be called the installation of " clean housekeeping methods ", as it was really no more than cleaning up rubbish accumulation of all kinds and installing the simplest devices, such as metal receptacles to hold waste paper in factories, metal covers for laundry tables and the elimination of swinging and unprotected gas fixtures in cellars and under stairways, etc.

In Philadelphia the following methods are used:

1. Inspectors call attention to defects immediately and have them remedied, if possible, before they leave the premises
2. In addition to calling attention to defects, inspectors leave a written memorandum with the occupant of matters to which they wish attention given. This is quite important, especially when the real owner or responsible person is not present during the inspection
3. The memorandum thus left with the occupant is followed up by an official notice from headquarters after the lapse of sufficient time for the occupant to correct conditions
4. Immediately afterwards a re-inspection is made to determine whether or not recommendations have been complied with

Inasmuch as the police and firemen of Milwaukee are under the same head, and since the police have power to enforce all ordinances and regulations, if necessary the orders sent by the fire department requiring persons to clean up their buildings might be countersigned by the chief of police.

Seventy per cent of the fires which comprised the $250,000,000 fire loss in the United States during 1912 had their origin in poor housekeeping methods, all easily preventable. Milwaukee has an annual per capita fire loss of $2.20, stated by the Board of Fire Underwriters to be moderate, but it is considerably higher than it would be were more extensive precautionary methods used.

Sketches of Large Buildings

One purpose of the inspections made by district chiefs is to familiarize themselves with the internal arrangements of buildings. Except in a few instances no sketches are made so that information obtained is not available for the general use of the company. For all large establishments sketches should be prepared showing methods of ingress and egress, the location of elevators, fire escapes, special fire appliances, etc., and whether a sprinkler system is installed and in what parts of the building, and what, if any specially inflammable material is customarily kept on the premises, etc.

Preventable Fires in Milwaukee

The annual report for 1911 shows a total of 1,685 alarms. Of these 696 were due to easily preventable causes, provided the public is taught the importance of caution. Examples of these preventable causes are: chimney fires 121, carelessness with matches or fire 110, oily rags and waste 30.

To prevent fires the fire department should conduct an educational campaign similar to the campaign conducted by the health department to prevent disease.

Chief Should Have Greater Power

The fire chief should have power to enforce preventive measures, as broad as those recently granted the fire chief (commissioner) in New York City. In New York, the commissioner personally or through his agents may:

1. Inspect any building, structure, inclosure, vessel, place or premises
2. Remedy any condition found in violation of any law or ordinance in respect of fires or the prevention of fires, except the tenement house law (enforced by the tenement house department)
3. Require the installation of automatic fire alarm systems, fire extinguishing equipment and adequate and safe means of exit
4. Require to be vacated any building or structure which in his opinion is inadequately protected against fire
5. Require a vessel anchored near any dock to be removed to a place designated by the commissioner, provided the vessel is on fire or in danger of catching fire, or from

97

the nature of its cargo a menace to the shipping property on the water-front

6. Require regular and periodical fire drills in factories stores, schools, hospitals and asylums, to declare a building deficient in fire extinguishing equipment or one which by reason of contents or overflowing is perilous to life and property, to be a nuisance, and to direct such nuisance to be abated

7. Direct, subject to review of the board of surveyors, the owner of such property within a reasonable time to place his building in a condition of safety, and if the owner fail, take the necessary steps to remove the dangerous condition

Fire Departments Backward

Fire departments have been less active in fire prevention work than chambers of commerce and other organizations with less direct responsibility for fire prevention. Some of these organizations have conducted effective anti-fire educational campaigns. Among these Rochester, N. Y., is conspicuous. The Rochester chamber of commerce gives the following advice to all manufacturers and owners of buildings:

1. " Study your place alone to note every fire-breeding condition

2. " Call in the fire marshal to make a similar study and to report his observations

3. " Call in the man who places your insurance and ask him to investigate and report

4. " Then concentrate first on the sources of danger noted in all three inspections and eliminate them

5. " Do not put your trust in a ' fire proof ' building—your responsibility is just as great as in a wooden structure

6. " Risks are dangerous or not, as the owners make them so. It isn't wholly the nature of the business. It is the nature of the men

7. " Study to *prevent* fires in your houses or place of business

8. " Be prepared to put fires out *before* they become dangerous

9. " Be prepared to save every person in your employ if your place burns—plan before the fire occurs

10. " ' It's none of my business ' doesn't apply to fires. Every fire is your business—it hits your pocketbook.

11. " Insurance will cover only a small part of your loss is you have a fire. Insurance is a partial payment, not an absolution

12. " Fire prevention is largely a matter of cleanliness and carefulness in the individual—in you "

By following the last precept, the Philadelphia fire department, through inspection by firemen, is rapidly cutting down Philadelphia's fire loss.

Fire prevention rather than fire fighting is the present day first duty of a progressive fire department.

District Maps in Fire Stations

Fire stations are not now provided with maps showing the district in which the company is called on first alarm. Such maps should be provided. These maps should indicate all information which would be of particular service in case of fire. Buildings in which combustibles are stored should be indicated. Poorly built buildings, etc., and the location of each water hydrant in the district should be indicated on the map.

Other Information Suggested

Each company should also be provided with a list of the buildings in its first alarm area, which are equipped with standpipes and sprinklers.

Motor Apparatus Urged

The city has practically no motor fire-fighting apparatus. The records indicate that horses are still being purchased although it is understood that the department intends to purchase motor-driven apparatus.

Fire departments throughout the country are fast realizing that motor apparatus is superior in every way to horse-drawn apparatus and in large part have already stopped purchasing horses.

Medical Examination

As in the case of the police department, candidates for admission to the fire force are not medically examined until after they have passed their written examination and are ready for appointment. As a result, men who have qualified in other respects are rejected at the last moment. A medical examination should be given when a man first applies for admission to the department in order to exclude the physically unfit. A second examination should be given before admission, as now, to determine whether any important physical defects have developed subsequent to the preliminary examination.

Defective Promotional System

In promotional tests service performance of the candidate is not taken into account nor the length of his service. Promotion is based entirely on written examination. This method of selecting men for advancement disregards a good fireman's most valuable asset, the capacity to fight fires.

The chief of the department disapproves of the present method of selecting men for promotion.

No Efficiency Records

An essential part of a good promotional system is an intelligently planned and well kept efficiency or service record. At present on the personal record kept of firemen, besides historical data such as date of admission, promotion, etc., only notes of fines, absences and delinquencies are made. No notation is made of service efficiency. Though reports are made on individual firemen by commanding officers, they are filed away and are rarely considered in determining promotions. Such records have not been considered or asked for by the board of fire commissioners.

Excellent Book of Rules

The department's manual of rules is comprehensive and well prepared. Except for needed amplification of certain rules relating to inspections and reports the manual is an excellent guide to the departmental routine.

HEALTH DEPARTMENT

Department Progressive

Judged by the report of 1911, the last report available, and our survey, the Milwaukee health department has a comprehensive program for protecting the public health. The range of its activities compares very favorably with the most progressive health departments in the country. In our brief survey we discovered many indications of efficiency.

Scientific health work in cities is a relatively modern development. No city has achieved perfect control over health conditions. It is not discreditable to Milwaukee, therefore, that there are still opportunities for improving the efficiency of its health service. These will be briefly referred to, in full appreciation of the fact that against them can be placed a large number of activities which are conspicuously creditable. Because of the interesting and vital character of this department's work we very greatly regret that time did not permit a full study of health problems in Milwaukee and a more detailed analysis of the activities of the department.

More Funds Needed

With the evident present understanding of public health needs in Milwaukee, it should be possible to obtain for the health department adequate power and adequate funds to improve the public health service. Including an allowance of $37,050 for hospitals, the total appropriation for the health department for 1913 is $157,320.83 or forty-two cents per capita.

The health bulletin for March makes the following statement:

> "Cities ranging from 30,000 to 50,000 in population should have a minimum per capita cost of 50 cents; cities ranging from 50,000 to 100,000 should have a minimum cost per capita of 75 cents; cities from 100,000 to 300,000 should have a minimum cost per capita of 85 cents; and all cities over 300,000 population should have not less than one dollar per capita."

A Special Health Ordinance Body

There is no board of health in Milwaukee. Health ordinances are passed by the common council after reference to the aldermanic committee on health. Unless the council as a whole is peculiarly well-informed regarding health matters, it is not likely that so large a body will prove sufficiently aggressive in the preparation of health ordinances.

It is suggested that a health board be established with power to frame and adopt a sanitary code and special health regulations.

While the law may not require that the commissioner of health devote his entire time to the service, it has, nevertheless, become customary for the commissioner to devote virtually all his time to his office. It is improbable that the practice of giving only partial time will ever again become established. It would be a safeguard to make it a provision of law that the head of the health department shall devote his full time to his public position.

A Full Time Staff

There are approximately 100 employees in the health department. Of these, in addition to the commissioner, only five are physicians who are known as assistant commissioners of health. The assistant commissioners receive salaries of $50 a month and are subject to the call of the department. Their duties involve the diagnosis of contagious cases and attendance at the city hospital.

The department should employ as assistants to the commissioner at least five physicians at full time, in order that they may give their entire attention to intensive study and direction of health department work.

Contagious Disease Control

In 1911, 3,832 cases of scarlet fever, diphtheria and other contagious diseases, exclusive of tuberculosis, were reported to the department. Physicians are required to report all cases of contagious diseases, and, thereafter, except in measles cases, inspection is made by the health department in order to enforce quarantine. These inspections are made not by physicians or nurses, but by sanitary inspectors who are unable to render any practical service to families requiring it. Quarantining, however, is only a small part of a progressive health department's responsibility in contagious cases.

Diagnoses are not confirmed except in the case of diphtheria where cultures are analyzed by the department's bacteriological laboratory.

Sanitary inspectors are not equipped to advise parents as to means of avoiding contagion, or to render the helpful assistance of which a visiting nurse would be capable.

Control over contagious cases is modified by a rule of the department which exempts a householder in whose home a contagious disease occurs from the daily visit of the inspector, provided he will in writing discharge the department from its legal responsibility. It is stated that over 50% of the householders avail themselves of this opportunity to assume in the department's behalf responsibility for protecting the public from the spread of contagious disease.

The commissioner stated that a year's observation of this discharge system has failed to indicate that it induces the breaking of quarantine or is in any sense harmful.

It is suggested that the educational work upon which the department relies for results in the control of tuberculosis and infantile diarrhea be extended to this division, and that one or two nurses be assigned to visit homes in which children are reported sick from a contagious disease. It should be the duty of these nurses to instruct the parents in prophylactic methods.

Supervision should be exercised over the return of children to school. Free medical service should be provided for children of indigent parents who are unable to provide them with medical attention.

There is no compulsory vaccination in Milwaukee. If a smallpox case occurs in school, children may either be vaccinated or leave school for 21 days.

Effective Laboratory Work

The most effective work done in the control of contagious diseases is in the bacteriological laboratory. Diagnosis is made of diphtheria, typhoid fever, tuberculosis and of ophthalmia neonatorum.

To assist physicians in submitting cultures for examination, culture stations have been established all over the city from which collections are made daily by the sanitary inspectors.

103

In the laboratory routine examination of the city drinking water is made. It was stated by the bacteriologist that pathogenic germs are found in increasing numbers in the water, due to the growing amount of sewage emptied into the lake.

Serum Distribution Should Be Extended

Free diphtheria antitoxin vaccine is provided for the use of physicians in treating indigent patients. The important place that serums are taking in the control of disease makes it desirable that the health department should encourage their use by liberal distribution of the serums and their expert administration.

To develop this branch of prevention and treatment, it would be necessary to keep the diagnostic work in a separate laboratory from the production, storing or administering of vaccines or serums.

Anti-Tuberculosis Work Effective

Progressive work is being done by the department in fighting tuberculosis.

An index file is kept for the registration of living cases and through coöperation with physicians, private clinics, visiting nurses, other organizations and the public, an increasing number of cases are being registered. The very difficult and perplexing task of keeping track of patients, frequently moving from place to place, is solved by intelligent coöperation with the police department.

Upon the evidence of records seen in the office of the division high praise must be given to the service of the visiting nurses. The day's work is planned in conference with the supervisor and is reported with sufficient detail at the end of the day. Nursing as well as instruction is given to families visited. Preventive work is done by examining and supervising the non-infected members of the family, and by removing incipient cases, whenever possible, to the city sanitarium at Blue Mounds.

Power of Forcible Removal Desirable

Information was obtained that adequate hospital facilities will be provided for advanced cases in the near future. It is probable that Milwaukee will find it desirable to give its health department the power of forcible removal in order to control in the tuberculosis hospital the cases most dangerous to the community.

Tuberculosis Clinic Needed

Admirable as is the present beginning of the control of tuberculosis, it cannot be considered complete until the department either establishes a tuberculosis clinic of its own, or exercises some form of control over private clinics now existing. For many years to come Milwaukee cannot expect to send all incipient cases to a sanitarium. A clinic would be useful in inviting early diagnosis and in establishing some control of the treatment of cases at home.

Medical Inspection of School Children

Medical inspection of school children in the public schools is under the supervision of the school board. Parochial schools are not generally subjected to medical supervision and an offer of inspection was accepted by only four schools. In 1911 an examination was made by the health department of 4,000 children. The children of four parochial schools were also examined in 1912, but there has not been established a systematic inspection of parochial school children. For their own sakes, as well as for the sake of the community, whose health they affect, these children should receive health department supervision.

A Resident Physician for the Isolation Hospital

The city maintains an isolation hospital of 100 beds for contagious diseases. About one-third of the contagious cases reported are sent to this hospital. The hospital is under the jurisdiction of a matron superintendent. No resident physician is in attendance, medical service being supplied by the assistant health commissioners, who for periods of one month, are in succession, made responsible for hospital cases.

A resident physician should be stationed in the hospital and the matron relieved from full responsibility for medical attention in the absence of the visiting physician.

Midwives Should Be Supervised

Midwives are required to register in the same manner as physicians, so that the department is in a position to exercise supervision over them. Over 50% of reported births are assisted by midwives. The need for supervision is indicated by a large number of cases of ophthalmia neonatorum discovered by nurses at baby stations. All midwives should be subjected to regular inspection, and instructed by department representatives in hygienic practices.

Birth Records Not Checked

No attempt is made to check the completeness of birth reports. A good beginning in making such a check would be to locate in the files of births the names of babies visited by the nurses of the child welfare division.

Milwaukee's health department cannot afford to use as its basis of health control, and as the test of its success, vital statistics that are merely the tabulation of voluntarily offered information. Physicians and midwives must be made to realize the value of reports, and to comply with the law relating thereto.

According to the commissioner of health, such educational efforts are being undertaken, both through the department's regular publications and, more directly, by means of circular and personal letters. It is claimed that several thousand such letters were forwarded to Milwaukee physicians during the past year.

Food Inspection Commendable

The department has established active supervision of stores where food is sold. Before granting a license to sell, the department inspects and scores the conditions found. Through re-inspections the continuance of sanitary conditions is enforced.

In the case of bake shops the department has devised a system of control by keeping the records of scoring and inspection of each bakery on an individual card. This history card gives definite information of the efficiency of supervision. In case of other food stores, only the orders issued to the storekeeper when violations of health regulations are found are reported, but not the number and dates of inspections.

Inadequate Slaughter House Control

The conditions under which animals are allowed to be slaughtered in Milwaukee make an effective control of slaughter houses very difficult. As there are 18 separate slaughtering houses to be inspected, and as licensed butchers are permitted to slaughter calves and sheep, a thorough inspection of all meat would appear to be impossible with the staff provided.

If Milwaukee suffers the experience of other cities, it will find that beef which cannot pass the federal inspector or which the shipper fears will not pass, is shipped into the slaughter houses for the local market. The need of vigorous inspection of slaughter houses for the local market is therefore increased. Milwaukee must either provide for the slaughtering of all animals under one roof, or largely increase its inspection staff.

The chief food inspector has suggested that a municipality owned or municipality controlled slaughter house be erected and that slaughtering be prohibited except on these premises.

The department has the coöperation of the courts in the enforcement of the food laws. It has far less difficulty in this respect than in enforcing sanitary and communicable disease measures.

Inspection of Milk Supply

Farm inspection should be extended. Milwaukee's milk is received from some 2,500 farms. In 1911 only 126 farms were inspected and scored. The condition of cows and stables determines in a very large degree the purity and safety of the milk

107

a city receives. Farm inspection is of the greatest importance. Funds should be provided to enable the department to control effectively the sources of milk supply, or an effort should be made to get the state to do it adequately.

The farm inspection of the past has been carried out virtually at the expense of the inspectors assigned to the work. They have been required to use a part of their salary to cover traveling expenses. Since such expenses are comparatively large, farm inspection is, necessarily, entirely too restricted. The chief milk inspector is requesting an adequate appropriation for this work.

To supplement the work of the inspectors the dairymen are periodically reminded to keep the milk and the milk cans clean. A department inspector puts a label on one or two cans of every milk shipper about once a month when cans are returned to the producer. This label advises the dairymen to feed their cows clean, wholesome food; keep barns well lighted and ventilated; thoroughly clean and scald utensils daily; clean and whitewash the barn and keep it clean. Milk into a small-top pail; cool milk promptly to 50 degrees or lower, and finally store milk in clean milk houses.

Labels warning customers to clean milk bottles immediately after emptying are distributed by the department to milk dealers, to be put on bottles going to careless customers.

Effective Coöperation of Milk Dealers

Fifty per cent. of Milwaukee's milk supply is milked into "three-quarters closed-top pails", and the percentage is rapidly increasing. The small-top pail reduces by 75% the surface into which filth may fall during the process of milking.

This result was brought about by the energetic efforts of the inspectors to teach the dairymen the practical advantages of this type of pail.

Refrigeration Cars Not Required

Milk in transit to the city is under the jurisdiction of state laws. These do not require railroads to provide refrigerator cars for milk. Consequently, in summer, milk often reaches the city overheated.

Bacterial Tests Valuable the Year Round

Bacteriological examinations of milk are made to determine the presence of disease bearing germs and to test cleanliness. In 1911, 768 bacteriological examinations were made. In 1911, 2,171 milk dealers' licenses were issued. Obviously, bacteriological tests were not made of milk handled by all these dealers. Of the 768 bacterial tests made, 618, or 80% were made in the months of July and August.

July and August are generally the months of greatest danger from bacterial contamination of milk. To limit bacteriological tests of milk to the months of July and August is, however, undesirable, because dealers, knowing that practically no tests will be made during the remainder of the year, are likely during that time to exercise less care in protecting their milk from contamination. Moreover, infant mortality prevention work of June and May is not aided as it would be by current bacteriological reports on the milk supply.

Periodical publicity should be given to all milk tests, and all reports thereon should state the dealer's name and should contain explanations of the importance and meaning of the findings.

A Commendable Step

The sale of "loose" milk is prohibited and all milk sold in stores must be bottled. This is an excellent requirement provided the public does not assume that milk is clean because it is bottled.

Milk Ungraded

The health department has established no grades of milk, the same standards being imposed for milk used for cooking as for milk used for infant feeding. Milk should be graded so as to raise the standards of milk for infant feeding, while dealing less rigorously with milk to be used for cooking purposes. A producer who takes special care in the selection of the stock and in the sanitary condition of his supply, is now required to compete with the dealer whose supply of milk is far inferior, but still within minimum standards. There is now an agreed national standard which with slight, if any modification, is immediately applicable to Milwaukee.

The chief milk inspector says that the matter of graded milk has already been discussed in some detail with the dealers of Milwaukee and, furthermore, he claims that a suggestion for a milk ordinance was recently presented to the common council for consideration. This bill provided for the establishment of graded milk, but it was not passed. We have not examined the proposed ordinance.

Infant Mortality and Systematic Inspection of Baby Homes

In 1911, 1,217 deaths as against 10,829 births occurred among infants under one year of age, or at the rate of 112 deaths per 1,000 living infants under one year. As compared with other cities this rate is not excessive. Many of these lives, however, could have been saved by proper care and feeding.

Preventive work begun by the child welfare commission will lower this record.

The work of the nurses who visit infants would be greatly facilitated if steps were taken to advertise it more extensively.

A very effective way of advertising this work is by supplying, at cost, milk for infants or for nursing mothers at the child welfare stations. The supply of milk at the stations will attract the mothers; and many babies can be seen by the nurse at the station, thus saving her time in visiting or enabling her to visit other babies living too far from the station to be brought to it.

Attractive posters, giving simple directions and advertising the child welfare work, could be distributed by school children. Greater publicity as to the location of stations through the coöperation of the newspapers, schools, teachers, etc., could undoubtedly be obtained.

The city has no maternity hospital, but the health department through licensing exercises some supervision over 26 private baby farms and maternity institutions.

These neighborhoods need attention.

A nurse has recently been assigned to the supervision of these boarded children.

Inspection of Complaints

Complaints of nuisances are received at the desk of the chief sanitary officer. Complaints from citizens are referred to an inspector to be investigated the day after they have been received. If a nuisance is found by the inspector, he issues a written request for its abatement, which is immediately sent to the party responsible. A copy of this request is filed with the chief for future action.

All complaints are recorded by the chief clerk and the book of complaints kept by him furnishes a complete history of action taken. A double check is therefore kept upon the proper disposal of complaints, both by the chief sanitary officer and by the clerk.

Complainants, however, should be informed of results of inspection and action taken by the department in pursuance of complaints made by them. Only a small portion of the complaints are made by citizens, and the habit of complaining should be encouraged by extending every courtesy to the complainant.

Housing Control

A cursory inspection of housing conditions in the neighborhood of two of the baby welfare stations indicated that Milwaukee has not escaped the tenement problem. The following are only scattered examples of conditions observed. On Cherry Street there is a row of three double tenements facing the street. Separating the buildings are alleys not more than three feet wide. The only light and air that could reach the windows of the middle rooms comes from this narrow alley. In the rear of the building lot and only a short distance from the buildings are three duplicates of the front houses. In the alley between the houses garbage and refuse were dumped in profusion. Only one garbage can was in evidence and that was overflowing. A drain in the center of the yard was filled with potato peels.

In three or four double tenements which were observed, the central hallway separating the apartments is so narrow that two people can hardly pass each other. In one house this central hall is broken in the middle by a spiral stairway—a well-designed fire trap.

The rear alley, badly paved, with broken wooden manure boxes, garbage and ashes thrown about, was conspicuous. One wooden garbage box was seen near the sidewalk in front of the building.

Middle and rear lot dwelling houses with water closets in the yards are common. Complaints are frequently made that the water has not been running in the closets for weeks.

In one outlying section recently built up the underground basement was found in many of the houses. In these underground rooms people lived. A number of infants were seen in them. In many the floors were rotting and full of holes and cracks.

A Health Department Task

The blame for these building conditions cannot be laid upon the present health department. But the city should look to the department for the intelligent planning to prevent the increase of these and similar conditions, and to propose steps for the speedy elimination of unnecessary dangers. There should be a systematic inspection of tenement houses.

Information as to housing conditions found by inspectors is not now recorded by the department in such manner as to make it valuable in city planning or in the agitation for a modern building code.

Tenements are not subjected to systematic inspection, and living apartments, except in basements, are not inspected except on complaint. The health department should supervise the construction and alteration of buildings in order to insure proper provision for light and air.

Factory Inspection

Factories are inspected and the coöperation with the state industrial commission in the enforcement of orders is apparently cordial.

Privy Vaults Should Be Abolished

In 1911 there were still remaining 1,200 privy vaults in out-lying districts not yet provided with sewers. Vaults are a fertile source of disease, and the health department should obtain the coöperation of the commissioner of public works in providing, as promptly as possible, sewers for the districts now without them.

Smoke Nuisance

Considerable attention to the smoke nuisance is given in the annual report for 1911. Smoke suppression is not under the health department, but under a special smoke inspector. A casual inspection of the city showed that many plants and buildings were emitting black smoke.

Bureau of Education and Publicity

Special mention should be made of the excellent educational work conducted for the past several years by the department. The monthly and special bulletins in " Healthology " are interestingly prepared. Occasionally special articles are not well timed. Thus, an article on the " hokey pokey " man, a particular danger of the summer months, appeared in March. The bulletin would be more directly helpful if, each month, suggestions especially pertinent to that month and its dangers were furnished. At the end of each number of the bulletin health statistics for the month are given. It would be helpful if the significance of the tables were lucidly explained in the text of the report.

Attention Given to Records

A study of the records of the department reveals that a process of systematizing records is under way. It is evidently the pur-pose of the new system to collate in one place all information relating to any case, store or place under supervision.

An excellent example of a consolidated record is the bakery score card previously mentioned. The intention was expressed to prepare a record of this kind for places covered by food and milk inspection; similarly for contagious disease control. All records relating to a particular family will be filed together if a communicable disease has been found therein.

Records of infants visited, of the number of visits made and conditions found are kept in the office of the child welfare commissioner. The records now kept are indispensable for the correct estimation of the value of the work done and in modifying and improving present plans.

Daily Reports Lacking

Only from the nurses visiting tubercular cases are adequate daily reports of work performed demanded. This method of rendering daily reports should be required in all departments. A form of daily report could readily be devised by which each inspector would account for his time as well as give detailed information of services rendered. This daily report could be used by the office clerk in recording the inspections made of each store or place under supervision. As it is, the chief food inspector, for instance, cannot tell how many inspections have been made of any one store. A record of inspection is now made only when cause for issuing an order is found.

Advantage of Daily Report System

A detailed daily report would not necessarily increase the clerical work of the inspector as it would take the place of many of the individual reports now made. It would give the supervising officer a picture of the daily work of the staff which the monthly summary of the number of services performed cannot now present. It would enable him to plan a more economical performance of present work.

An Excellent Health Report

The 1911 report of the department is interestingly prepared and sets a standard for future departmental reports.

In addition to the tables now published, some of which the department will doubtless care to modify in the interest of

Some day this railroad will be covered, permitting the park to stretch down to the lake shore.

clearness, it is suggested that operation statistical tables be devised of the department's activities. Each table should show specifically, work done, action taken and results obtained. This information is not always shown in the tables in the health report.

Even if the department should assign to the bureau of information and publicity a competent assistant to perfect the system of supervisory records, the increased efficiency resulting therefrom would warrant the expense.

Emergency Hospital

A brief examination of the emergency hospital indicated that it was well conducted. The hospital is, however, in urgent need of a new building. The present building, because of internal construction and the shutting off of light and air by abutting buildings, is totally unfit for hospital purposes.

PARK BOARD

A Single Head for the Parks

The independent park board, by protecting the city from politics in land purchases, doubtless served a useful purpose during the time that acquisition of park lands was the principal function of the park department. But the present function of the department is increasingly administrative. As an administrative department it should be directed by a single executive responsible to the mayor. Executive functions are not now performed by the park board, but delegated with no specific prescription of duties to the secretary and the superintendent.

Opportunity for Wise Planning in Undeveloped Parks

According to the secretary of the park board, 338 out of 930 acres owned by Milwaukee for park purposes are partially or wholly undeveloped. There is a very large opportunity, therefore, for applying intelligent landscaping and planning for recreational use to a large part of the city's common grounds.

115

The city should have a comprehensive park and playground and boulevard plan laid out far in advance of immediate requirements. Studies already made of the park problems by landscape architects may be used, and if necessary, these should be extended. German cities, with which many Milwaukeeans are familiar, are now planning their park systems many years ahead. The city of Düsseldorf is laying plans for a fifty year park program.

One Road-Maker for Entire City

Park roads are built and maintained by the park department. Irrespective of the efficiency of present road work under the park department, there should be one road-building and maintenance agency for the entire city—the bureau of street construction and repair of the department of public works.

Why Two Police Departments?

The park police, now numbering 24 men, should be consolidated with the general city police and placed under the supervision of the police chief. Police funds may be reimbursed out of the park fund, for the cost of policing parks.

Applicants are admitted to the park police force up to 45 years of age. Admission to the general police force is limited to men under 32 years of age.

Centralize Buying

The park department makes all its own purchases. Supplies required by the park board should be bought by the central purchasing division in the department of public works. As an alternative an analysis should be made at once of supplies regularly required by the parks and, on the basis of quantities consumed during the past year, contracts should be executed for all supplies regularly required. Supplies are now bought in small quantities as needed, irrespective of total amounts used in a year.

Preserve and Increase Street Trees

Street trees should be placed under the care of the park department. A 1911 law giving the department this control has

Milwaukee has miles of shaded residence streets. These trees should be protected by constant care.

been held defective by the city attorney on a verbal opinion, because the cost of tree care was to be assessed against private property owners. No attempt was made to obtain a revision of the law at the last session of the legislature. Street trees are a valuable city asset. If necessary they should be planted and cared for out of general city funds.

Educational work has not been done either through the schools or otherwise to prevent the neglect or misuse of grass plots and trees on streets.

Creditable Accounting Work

Commendable steps have been taken to improve the accounts of the department, and for this the secretary deserves credit. As yet, however, no accounting control is exercised over stores and equipment, and accounts are on a cash instead of a liability basis. These defects can easily be remedied. When accounts are kept on the basis of liabilities incurred instead of disbursements, the secretary's excellent expenditure reports will be made more useful.

Useful Data Not Yet Supplied

Comparative per acre maintenance costs are not kept for the several parks, nor are square yard or mileage costs kept for park road maintenance.

Inadequate Lighting

Naphtha lamps are now used to light the parks. Arc lights should be installed in all parks frequented at night.

Advertisement of Park Privileges

Park privileges for the operation of refreshment stands, etc., are not advertised, but are granted for three-year periods to persons selected by the park board. This method is used to control the character of wares supplied by privilege holders. Competition would doubtless bring a larger revenue from park privileges. Better control over the purity of wares would be obtained if the health department were called upon to inspect periodically all food stuffs sold in parks.

A City Repair Shop

The department makes only minor repairs to equipment, important repairs being made on open market order. It would probably be profitable for the city to maintain a repair shop where all equipment including that of parks, public works, etc., could be repaired. As suggested with reference to the bureau of sanitation, the repair shop of the fire department could doubtless be expanded to answer all the city's needs.

BUREAU OF WEIGHTS AND MEASURES

Bureau Seems Efficient

From a brief examination weights and measures work in Milwaukee seems to be efficiently conducted.

Additions to Ordinance Suggested

A new ordinance passed in 1909, plus a state law, is the basis for the bureau's work. This ordinance, while excellent in many particulars, does not give the sealer certain powers which are essential to most effective work. The following additions are suggested:

1. The sealer is not given the power to destroy defective apparatus, except after a ten days' notice to repair. He should be empowered to condemn, and destroy outright, apparatus beyond repair or deliberately falsified

2. "Condemned" tags affixed to disapproved and incorrect scales state that they may not be removed on penalty. The ordinance, however, seems to provide no penalty. A penalty of $25 should be provided for an unauthorized removal of a "condemned" tag

3. The sealer should have power for publicly stated reasons to exclude undesirable types of weights and measures from use in Milwaukee. Certain types though prima facie honest are especially susceptible of fraudulent use. The state sealer now has this power and the city sealer operates under it. The city sealer should have specifically conferred upon him power to exclude undesirable types

In this connection the first deputy sealer of Milwaukee writes as follows:

" Although our ordinance does not give the sealer the right or power to forbid the sale of certain types of scales we have the regulations of the state superintendent of weights and measures to work under. These regulations are similar to those in effect in New York State —in fact I think they were copied from the New York regulations and specifications. So you see we are passing on practically the same types that are passed on in New York, and we handle the subject in a less expensive manner, and probably just as efficiently.

" Our ordinance requires that all scales must be sealed before they can be used in this city. We have instructed all agents and dealers that they must sell scales with the understanding that if they do not pass the inspection of the sealer they may be returned and the money refunded to the purchaser. If a scale is purchased and reported to this office, and if the inspector finds that it does not fulfill our requirements, he tags it ' condemned ' and gives the reason on the tag for condemning it. If the scale happens to be one of the kind that is prohibited, the dealer returns it to the factory and informs the manufacturer that he cannot buy any more scales of that type in the future."

4. The ordinance should require owners of scales to display in a conspicuous place certificates of inspection

5. Peddlers are now licensed by the state. It is impossible for the local authorities to revoke the licenses of peddlers convicted of short weighing or measuring. This power should be conferred by statute

Further Information Suggested for Dealers' Register

A card register of dealers and establishments using weights and measures is kept. In addition to the information at present provided for, there should be recorded: the number and character of all weighing and measuring instruments in the establishment, the name of the inspector testing and reporting on them, the results of inspection with the character of violation found, if any. Under character of violation there should be given sufficient detail to indicate whether the violation was due to carelessness, such as unclean scales, scales slightly out of repair, weather conditions, etc., or to fraud. Tabs attached to the cards should indicate violations found. Tabs of different colors should be used to show at a glance whether violations were due to carelessness or to fraud. A housewife about to select her tradesman in a new neighborhood into which she has moved, upon making inquiry at the bureau of weights and measures, would go to the filing case containing the record cards of the tradesmen of her locality. A glance would tell her their weights and measures character. If this system were put into operation it would not be long before tradesmen would vigorously strive to keep their record cards in the bureau free of a fatal tab.

Changes in Forms

Condemnation tags should, for impressiveness, bear the seal of the city. Those used in sections occupied by foreign speaking people should be printed in foreign languages.

To facilitate control over the use of seals, seal tags should be numbered serially and a record made of the number used.

The certificate of inspection should be worded as follows:

> " This is to certify that the scales, weights and
> measures of ....
> street ....business ....
> ....have this..........day of..........,
> ....been examined and found to be as indicated
> below," etc.

Forms of dealers' report of scales and measures in use should provide for a schedule of weights used.

Inspectors' report slips bear no titles indicating the purpose for which they are used and do not provide for certification of facts contained in them.

Annual Report of Bureau

The annual report of the bureau of weights and measures should be most carefully prepared because information of weights and measures conditions is of the highest interest to the public. The sealer claims that sufficient funds are not provided to permit the publication of an adequate report. However this may be, the 1911 report does not do justice to the work of the bureau. The following suggestions are offered with regard to it:

Degree of Inaccuracy Not Shown

Tables are given showing the number of scales and measures found incorrect, but no information is given of the degree of inaccuracy or dishonesty. No differentiation is made between inaccuracies due to carelessness and those due to corrupt practices. Thus, if 100 spring balance butcher scales were found to be more than one-quarter pound fast, this would be a condition indicating wholesale fraud. If 100 platform coal scales were found to be one-quarter pound fast, it is hardly likely that the error would be traceable to fraud.

Number of Scales and Measures Destroyed Not Reported

The report contains a picture of condemned scales, but gives no information as to the number of scales and weights and measures confiscated.

The report gives no information on various means discovered of practicing fraud in weights and measures. Information of this kind should be furnished the public, in order that it may be forewarned. Not to give it is to lose to a large degree the educational opportunity afforded by the publication of the report.

Other Reporting Suggestions

The following tables, none of which is now included in the report, would be illuminating and help the sealer more effectively to present the results of his work to the public:

1. A table of places inspected by character of business, including the following headings:
   Character of business
   Total number of inspections
   Number of violations found
   Number of inspections where no violations were found
   Penalties imposed
   Arrests made
   Convictions had in criminal cases
   Cases where more than one violation was discovered in a year

   Under the first heading should be included
   Bakers
   Butchers
   Butter dealers
   Caterers
   Coal dealers
   Coal wagons
   Produce commission merchants
   Candy and confectionery
   Milk and cream dairies
   Delicatessens
   Drug stores
   Dry goods
   Feed and grain
   Fruits
   Fish, etc.

2. A table showing promiscuous peddler and huckster inspections as differentiated from stores and regular mercantile establishments. Inspections of pushcarts and hucksters in the field are made so quickly and with such little difficulty that a proper impression of the efficiency of the bureau is not given if they are included in a general table of inspections. A combined table does not enable the reader to determine whether fraud or carelessness is greater among peddlers than it is among storekeepers

3. A table showing tests made of institutional and city department scales

4. A table showing classification of apparatus, number of each type condemned and notice of violations filed
5. A table showing apparatus " confiscated and destroyed " as well as condemned—a term used in Milwaukee in the sense of " disapproved "
6. A table showing number and classification of new scales, weights and measures sealed during the year. This table would show the number of new apparatus coming into use, bringing added responsibility and work to the bureau
7. A comparative table by years showing number of routine inspections made, as against special inspections. By routine inspections is meant the annual inspection required by ordinance as against the special inspections required because of installation of new apparatus or suspicion or complaint of citizens
8. A table of purchases made for the purpose of testing, not the scales, but the manipulation of the scales, and the results found. This table should also show the amount of money spent by the bureau and its inspectors in purchase, as well as the disposition of the commodities purchased. For example, if an inspector purchased a ham for the purpose of testing the honesty of the butcher, this table should show the cost of the ham and the disposition made of it—whether it was turned over to a city institution or hospital, etc.
9. A table showing the number of tests made of packing companies' products and results of such tests
10. A table of complaints received and action taken
11. A table showing number of household weighing equipments tested upon request. The purpose of this table would be to show the number of families equipped with scales for their own protection
12. A table showing the number of inspections made by each inspector or deputy, arranged by months; the number of violations and condemnations made; arrests; convictions; penalty or fines imposed. Such a table should include the following headings:
    Inspector's name
    Total number of inspections made
    Number of articles condemned
    Number of violations
    Amount of money collected
    Number of arrests
    Dispositions

13. A table showing, by classification of business, the number of inspections and violations in public markets
14. Tables showing under classification as to business and apparatus violations where actual fraud was practiced, classified as follows:
    Tampering with a scale
    Fraudulent instrument
    Operators of scales detected manipulating

BOARD OF CITY SERVICE COMMISSIONERS

Civil Service in Milwaukee Selective But Not Protective

All civil service employees, except police and firemen, are removable at pleasure. Since 1911 removing officers must file with the city service board reasons for removal. These must not be political or religious. The removed employee may file an answer but he is given no hearing and has no day in court.

Removals of the clerical and technical forces are extensively made with changes in administration occurring every two years. This breaking up of the working forces nullifies one of the chief advantages of the merit system, namely, the development of a fairly permanent and experienced corps of departmental employees. All employees should be given notice of intended removal with a brief statement of reasons and afforded an opportunity to be heard in explanation of charges. A copy of the notice and answer should be filed with the city service commission. This measure would tend to give competent employees permanent tenure of position.

Defective Control of Civil Service Positions

The commission has established a classification of the official (non-labor) service modeled on the Chicago classification. It has no way of learning, however, whether employees are actually engaged on work for which they were examined. Titles and actual duties should be stated on payrolls, so that the commission may check all payrolls before payment to make certain that classified employees are engaged on work in conformance with their titles.

City Service Board Should Test Police and Fire Applicants

The police and fire board conducts competitive examinations for police and firemen. The city service board has no jurisdiction over these departments. It selects policemen, however, for the park department. There should be one civil service board for the city and it should be competent to select all city employees.

Appointments Should Be Made in Order of Certification

Appointing officers are not obliged to appoint in the order in which names are certified to them by the city service board, but a choice of several names is allowed. Names rejected three times are stricken from the list. This practice makes juggling of lists possible. Persons certified should be appointed in the order of their standing and dismissed if on probation they prove incompetent. Mayor Gaynor in New York has for three years with good effect insisted on selection in the order of certification.

Promotions Not Controlled

Promotions must be made subject to the approval of the city service board. The board does not, however, utilize its powers of approval to provide tests for promotion, either by means of examination or efficiency records.

With the present graded classification of the "official" service, the way is open to establishing an excellent promotional plan.

Efficiency Records Should Be Established

Efficiency records should be prescribed and kept in all departments, and periodical ratings communicated to the city service board.

Transfers Without Examination

Rule XVIII of the city service board permits the transfer of laborers who receive no examinations to the official class, members of which are appointed after examination. Though these transfers must be approved by the board, the power to make transfers of men selected without examination to positions properly filled by competition is the power to circumvent the civil service law.

Too Wide Discretion in Rejecting Laborers

Foremen appointing laborers have full discretion in determining the fitness of persons certified. They may reject any person who does not satisfy them. In order to make appointments of men of their own selection, foremen sometimes exhaust the certified list and make so-called " emergency " appointments. It sometimes happens that a foreman will have more " emergency " than certified laborers. This condition will continue until the city service board raises its present standards for laborers.

Power to Inquire Not Exercised

The commission has full power, and by law it is made its duty, to investigate the enforcement of the civil service law and regulations, and the duties and service of civil service employees. This power is not exercised, although by means of inquiry the commission could determine whether its examinations are designed to select competent men and eliminate the unfit. The commission should study departmental conditions continuously in order that it may adjust the whole civil service machinery to the practical requirements of departmental efficiency.

SUGGESTED NEXT STEPS FOR INCREASING THE EFFICIENCY OF MILWAUKEE'S CITY GOVERNMENT

Uncertainty of Official Efficiency Program

Admirable as are the present efforts of the mayor, the comptroller and other city officials to organize the business methods of the government on a sound basis, this work will not result in lasting departmental efficiency unless it is joined with public understanding of why it is necessary, and public appreciation of the benefits that will result from it. A change in administration may lead to the discontinuance of the mayor's bureau of municipal research and an interruption of the efficiency work carried on by the deputy comptroller. Unless citizens are intimately in touch with these activities, they will not be prepared to prevent an undoing of much of the constructive work that is now under way. There is comparatively little continuity in the city government and without continuity of attention efficient practices will not be permanently established. This continuity, the citizens, the beneficiaries of governmental efficiency and the victims of inefficiency, must supply. Discontinuance of constructive work inside City Hall with a change of administration can be prevented if citizens, by organized effort, keep intelligently informed of constructive work undertaken, its purpose, method and effect.

Inside Agency Required

Unquestionably, it is of the greatest importance that there should be within the city government an expert agency such as the present bureau of municipal research, whose energies are entirely devoted to studying means of increasing the effectiveness of city work. No great organization, spending $8,000,000 a year, with thousands of employees, can possibly be efficient unless it analyze continuously the results it obtains and compares them with results obtained by similar organizations elsewhere. For a period of five years many times the number of employees in the present expert staff of the mayor's bureau of municipal research and the comptroller's office could profitably be engaged in instituting in Milwaukee practices of efficiency which are now common to great private organizations.

Citizen Understanding Necessary

Because Milwaukee's city government undergoes disorganization every two years, no matter how effective the present bureau's work may be, there is no assurance that it will continue past the first of April, 1914, unless among citizens as a whole there is as definite an understanding of city government needs as there is among the members of the present administration.

A Citizens' Bureau Should Be Established

However efficient an inside agency may be, its efficiency will be increased and protected by intelligent outside coöperation.

It is, therefore, recommended that there be established in Milwaukee a competently organized Citizens' Bureau of Public Efficiency. This bureau, non-political, impersonal and non-partisan, should equip itself to coöperate effectively with the experts inside the city government in executing a constructive program of administrative betterment. In addition, it should equip itself to conduct day by day a publicity, educational campaign, so that no citizen in Milwaukee with the slightest interest in the efficiency of his government will be with excuse for not knowing what steps Milwaukee's city government needs to take to enable it to render maximum service to the community.

Opportunities for Coöperation

Immediate coöperative opportunities for a citizens' efficiency bureau are the following:

1. Providing **expert assistance to the deputy comptroller in reviewing, formulating and installing a uniform system of accounts.** The accounting reorganization is fundamental to 90% of the administrative reorganization of government. It should be pressed with all vigor. It is extremely important that it should be completed before the conclusion of the present administration, because the administration as a whole desires and appreciates the importance of accounting reform. By spending from $3,000 to $5,000 for this work during the next six months, Milwaukee's citizens will make a contribution of immeasurable value to city efficiency

2. **Organizing public interest in the preparation of the annual city budget, and coöperating with the board of estimate in testing and analyzing departmental requests for next year's allowances.** However efficiently officials may prepare a budget they are

helped by expert analysis of requests and proposed allowances from an *outside* point of view.

Business men's organizations, women's clubs, civic clubs, churches, charitable and philanthropic societies, all should be urged to participate in budget discussion. Every important outside social activity relates to the work of one or another department of the city government. A citizens' bureau should seek to make the annual budget a definite program of municipal action and an occasion for periodic revision of the citizens' specific directions to government officials

3. **Inaugurating plans for charter revision at the next session of the legislature.** The present charter, if indeed the present conglomeration of laws can be called a charter, is conceived to inhibit action instead of to facilitate it. Practically every provision of the present charter was drawn in fear of official inefficiency and corruption

4. **Coöperating in public works betterment.** The citizens' bureau should take advantage of the desire of the present commissioner of public works to make his department a model of efficiency. For every process in public works a definite procedure should be prepared, outlining methods which will compel economy by establishing the most direct and effective means of work performance. Public works administration all over the country is receiving expert attention. By putting Milwaukee in touch with New York, Philadelphia and other cities where progressive steps are being taken, and by making a detailed study of the specific problems of Milwaukee, a citizens' bureau could help materially in promoting public works efficiency

5. **Helping in formulating a city plan.** Milwaukee needs a "look ahead" city plan. Milwaukee's fine location gives it exceptional opportunities for ad-

vantageous planning. Preliminary studies should be made of streets, traffic, parks, housing, and industrial equipment—factory location, etc. A recent law permits the establishment of "zones" for industrial establishments. Every dollar spent on improvement in the future should be spent in conformance with a city plan. "*Städtebau*" has become a science in Germany. Milwaukee, which has profited so much from German influence, should be willing to avail itself of a most conspicuous present day example of German skill and progressiveness

6. **Making a coöperative city-wide health study.** The health department has much progressive work to its credit. A citizens' bureau should be equipped to coöperate effectively with the health commissioner in promoting a broad constructive health program. The health department should take a position of active leadership in furthering all health activities. It should be adequately manned, organized on a full-time basis, and generously supported. A city-wide survey of conditions affecting the health of the community should be made, followed by a detailed study of present administrative methods of the health department. With the start already made, the health department of Milwaukee can readily be put in the front rank of American health departments. Through a progressive health program, more effectively than in any other way, can the interest of the rank and file of citizens be developed and kept alive in city government economy and efficiency

7. **Within the limitations of funds made available for its work, coöperating with the bureau of municipal research in making a comprehensive detailed study of the administration of every department.** This preliminary study should be followed up by a similar survey of departments not covered in this study,

and later by an intensive analysis of every department of the government. Before the conclusion of the present administration there should be in the hands of a disinterested citizen agency complete information on the organization and processes of the city government, and knowledge as to where administrative methods have been improved and are efficient, and where they are still in need of strengthening. With this information the Milwaukee citizens' bureau will be equipped to continue its coöperation with the city government or to insist, through publicity, that the next administration, " no matter who is elected ", carry forward constructive work already begun

A citizens' bureau should have guaranteed for five years a sum of not less than $12,000 a year

DEPARTMENTS NOT COVERED IN SURVEY

Because of lack of time and the preliminary nature of our survey the following departments and divisions of departments were not examined:

Art commission
Bureau of buildings and elevator inspection
Bureau of plumbing, department of public works
Bureau of rivers and harbors, department of public works
Bureau of smoke suppression
City attorney
City clerk
Examiners of stationary engineers
Free employment commission
Public library
Public museum
Water department (now part of the department of public works)

An additional reason for omitting the water department is the fact that that department has recently been placed under the supervision of the Wisconsin Utilities Commission.

INDEX

Lightning Source UK Ltd.
Milton Keynes UK
UKHW022152180321
380610UK00003B/211